Ghillie Başan was born in Glasgow and brought up in Kenya and Scotland. Following a degree in Social Anthropology at Edinburgh University, she taught English in Italy and Turkey, and has worked as a cordon bleu cook, ski instructress, journalist, restaurant reviewer, and publisher. She is the author of the highly acclaimed *Classic Turkish Cookery*, shortlisted for the Glenfiddich and Guild of Food Writers' Awards, and contributes regularly to the *Sunday Herald* and the *Sunday Tribune*. Her most recent title is *The Middle Eastern Kitchen*. She lives in her remote cottage in Glenlivet with her husband, two little children and two huge dogs.

The Moon's Our Nearest Neighbour

GHILLIE BAŞAN

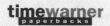
timewarner
paperbacks

A *Time Warner* Paperback

First published in Great Britain by Warner Books in 2001
Reprinted by Time Warner Paperbacks in 2003

A CIP catalogue record for this book
is available from the British Library.

ISBN 0 7515 3129 4

Typeset in Janson by M Rules
Printed and bound in Great Britain
by Clays Ltd, St Ives plc

Time Warner Paperbacks
An imprint of
Time Warner Books UK
Brettenham House
Lancaster Place
London WC2E 7EN

www.TimeWarnerBooks.co.uk

For Jonathan, without whom I couldn't live in the place of my dreams, and for Yasmin and Zeki, our two little gifts of life.

ACKNOWLEDGEMENTS

Life in the Braes of Glenlivet can be hard, but it would be a lot harder without the help and friendship of our triangle of neighbours – Norman and Jean Auchavaich, John and Mary Belnoe, and Hamish and Pam White. To them and to our friend Charlie Skene, who lends us tools and vehicles and helps to keep us on the road, we owe a big thank you. In a country community like this, there are so many characters to thank and mention, some who appear in the book, others who don't, but all contribute to the friendly spirit that makes this area such a pleasant place to live. So, really, I'd like to say a big thank you to everyone we know here.

To old friends far and wide, perhaps this book will go some way towards explaining our absences. I'd particularly like to mention David Allison, Liz and Ali Hunt, Alice and Sebastian Cooper, Alex and Anne Caroline Peckham, and Jerry and Alison Herman who invade our solitude with regularity and, uncomplainingly, muck in. And a special mention to John and Karon Hammond, who shared in the sweat, tears and gluttony of the early years and to Shan Singh, whose loo-reading found us the cottage in the first place.

If it wasn't for the unwavering faith and enthusiasm of our agent Giles Gordon, there probably wouldn't even be a book. When everything else seemed to be falling apart, both he and Susie Brumfitt kept our morale going. And behind every book there is a publisher. In this case, it was the most laid-back, friendly team I have ever come across. Barbara Boote, Joanne Coen, Louise Davies and the rest of the crew, whatever you're on I'd love some of it and thank you for taking me on.

I would also like to mention Ken Malcolm and Alistair Mitchell of the Bank of Scotland for boldly bearing with us. And last, but not least, we owe a great deal to both sets of parents.

One talks about everything in life in a way which shows that there is really nothing ordinary or mean on earth but all is extraordinary, and that the discovery of the extraordinary in the ordinary is more exciting than talking of the extraordinary . . .

Laurens Van der Post: *A Walk with a White Bushman*

The Move

The funny thing was we were only on this road because of a friend in London. Well, because of his bowel movements, to be precise. Sitting on the loo, flicking through the *Exchange & Mart*, he had spotted an advert for a remote cottage near Tomintoul. He had no idea where Tomintoul was. In fact, he had never heard of it. But he knew we were looking for a property in the highlands. 'Remote' sounded like the highlands. Anyway, he had reasoned, it was in Scotland. And Scotland was pretty wild. So he had phoned us with the details. I smiled to myself. What if he had picked up *Hello!*, his preferred choice of loo reading material?

Up and down, the road led us away from the picturesque order of Royal Deeside into the rest of the highlands. A hazardous road that never fails to bewitch me. It is arrestingly bleak. Broken shells of a few old dwellings lie testament to the fact that the bleakness had once been sparsely inhabited. Single trees stand on distant hills like lone soldiers. Grouse butts line the slopes with military precision. And, in the winter, this exposed single-track road is often blocked with snow.

I wondered why we hadn't looked for a property in this area before. We had been all the way to the north of the mainland. To Tongue, Loch Eriboll, and gusty Durness. Down the dramatic west coast to Lochinver, Glenelg, and the very tip of Ardnamurchan. We had even considered properties on Skye, Mull, and the outer isles. But we had completely neglected the hills of the eastern highlands and if ever there was a place that was natural for me to be, it was here in the wild fringes of the Cairngorms. In a sense, it was where I was from. Growing up, I had spent many happy holidays in this part of Scotland. Picnics by the Dee and swimming in the icy pools of the Lui and the Quoich, leisurely treks up Lochnagar and into the Cairngorms, whirling summer balls at Haddo House and, in the winters, blustery skiing on Glenshee's, often treacherous, slopes. For several generations, my father's family had been connected with the village of Braemar. In fact, he could almost be considered a local. And now retired from their Glasgow-based medical professions, he and my mother had turned the family holiday cottage into a full-time home. Not too far from the property we were about to see but far enough for familial comfort.

Coasting dreamily over the hilltops to Tomintoul, I was reminded of many family journeys on this very road.

Seated in the back, I would inevitably feel car-sick as we rode the numerous dips and turns. A lingering smell of mints and chocolate in the car would trigger off waves of nausea. My parents would remark that as a child I had travelled great distances in different parts of the world without ever feeling sick but, here, the twisty highland roads got me every time. The only cure, other than actually being sick, was to pull over regularly to let me walk and gulp in the fresh air. And then, installed in the back seat again, we would set off once more around the bends while my brother continued to guzzle a bar of Fry's chocolate mint cream.

Now years later, I found myself in the back seat again feeling just as car-sick, trapped under the warm weight of our big black dog, Biglie, who was comfortably slumped on top of me. In the front seat Liz, a friend visiting from London, was obliviously chewing through her packet of gum. She had been doing so since we left Edinburgh almost three hours ago and the smell of spearmint was beginning to overwhelm me with every twist in the road. So we had to pull over. Welcoming the opportunity, Liz scooted off to squat in the cover of a spindly wood while Jonathan embraced the chill air of the open moor and peed nonchalantly. The way men do. With Biglie dancing around me, I struck out across the tufts of heather concentrating on relieving the nausea. It was late March so there were still patches of snow on the ground. I scooped up a handful of fresh snow and pressed it on to my cheeks and forehead, circling it around my mouth to form a track of refreshing ice-cold droplets. I began to feel a little better, opening and closing my mouth like a fish to swallow the healing hill air deep into my lungs, and headed back to the car to resume my place as a cushion for Biglie, now wet from rolling in the snow. And, once again, trying to ignore the lingering smell of spearmint, I sank back into dreams of living in the hills.

A steep ascent took us right through the middle of the Lecht, a rather dejected-looking cluster of short, patchy ski runs, and on to the village of Tomintoul. The highest settlement in the highlands. 'Could be the Village of the Gauls,' Jonathan remarked with delight as we approached the line of low stone houses built on a plateau. Wisps of chimney smoke rose vertically above the village. A Gaulish hill retreat? I could picture it. Ready for battle or fishing, canoes bob at the banks of the River Avon below the village, the livestock graze in the lush pastures leading down to the curving Conglass where the women sing ballads while washing the clothes, Unhygienix sells rotten trout and rancid venison from his village stall, the wiry druid concocts his powerful magic potion from fermented grain and water in a copper still, while Asterix and Obelix, clad in their own eccentric tartan, hunt for wild boar in the woods. It may be reverie but I could bet that some of the characters existed.

The air was still and the smell of hot cooking fat hit us as we popped into the village store. Probably the haggis which, according to the sign outside, was 'freshly shot every morning'. Bleary-eyed and wise to in-comers, the bearded, pot-bellied owner stood by his extensive range of bottles. 'Aye, the best bloody whisky in the highlands,' he said with the conviction of a man who enjoyed more than a dram. 'Bloody good price too.' He didn't look like a man with whom you could haggle. He had a playful mischief in his eyes.

After the preliminary banter and a quick browse around the highland shop – oatmeal, dried fruits for baking, stacks of beer and whisky, and a delivery of fruit and vegetables on Thursdays – we told him where we were bound. 'People don't move *into* the Braes of Glenlivet,' he teased. 'They move *out*.' He pointed to the old black-and-white prints hanging above the counter – he and his father delivering groceries through a roof-high corridor of snow in the Braes. Only the chimneys poked out above the drifts. Admittedly, it was some twenty years ago but locals like to tease. By their very nature, in-comers are soft. They're not made of the real stuff. Porridge, peat and a fiery dram, that's what makes men hardy 'Aye, it's a cold, wild place,' he said, shaking his head as if in despair. 'If you can survive in the Braes, you can survive anywhere.'

We had just stepped into the dank, dingy pub, no more than a bar top with a stretch of dusty standing room when, mercifully, the estate agent turned up. It had been his idea to meet at this landmark, The Pole Inn,* about six miles

*recently changed hands

beyond Tomintoul. Carried away with the romance of the name, the three of us had conjured up an image of a big, open fire and home-made soup to warm the bellies of travellers. Not the impenetrable watering-hole of the local farmers. We nodded a hasty smile at the blank, ruddy-faced heads that had fixed silently on our entrance and swung around with relief.

We followed the agent's red Range Rover through the meandering glen to the Braes of Glenlivet. According to the local guidebook* we had picked up, the Braes 'were once the haunt of those "scandalous persons", cattle-reivers and whisky smugglers, and in the eighteenth century the refuge of oppressed Catholics'. We could see why. Tucked away at the foot of hills that backed into the Cairngorms, it was a dead-end glen. A lost world. Hills had to be crossed to go north, south, east or west. It had the look of a place left relatively unchanged with time. And untouched by the law. The kind of place where generation after generation the same family will farm the land. The kind of place that families don't leave too often so new blood rarely enters the chain. 'It's a terrible place,' one grouchy Tomintoul resident told us later. 'When God made the Earth, he made the Braes last.'

But as we approached the eye of the glen, the scene was benignly calm. Around us lay a scattering of farms in the midst of fields of bouncing calves and pregnant ewes, the old Catholic chapel, and a spanking whitewashed distillery

Avonside Explored by Edward H. Peck

which looked more like a Swiss château. Incongruous, perhaps, but not unexpected. We were, after all, in the heart of whisky country. It was hard to imagine the scene of 1746 when Hanoverian soldiers entered the glen and burnt down the Catholic seminary at Scalan. Where the priests, under the protection of the Dukes of Gordon, learnt geography, Greek and Hebrew and played shuttle-cock in their free time.

All of a sudden we turned off the road and on to a bumpy shooting track. Ahead of us, the agent cruised through a snow-drift but we, in our low-set Subaru Justy, came to an abrupt stop in the middle of it. We skidded out in reverse and transferred to the roomy comfort of the Range Rover. Only Biglie was rather miffed at the style in which he now found himself travelling – confined behind a dog barrier in the boot. The track seemed to go on and on, over pot-holes and through snow-drifts along the side of a dense plantation of spruce. Below us an untidy, muddy farm sprawled out across the bowl of the Braes. Old cars and tractors abandoned in fields, bales of rotting hay piled in tumbling heaps, twisted fences and their posts lying on the ground with large bits of plastic feed bag stuck to the wire. The scene could have been lifted from the obscure depths of rural West Virginia, only the mobile homes and trespassing signs were missing.

At the end of the plantation the track rolled down a slight descent and then gathered itself again in tight knots and ruts which led us through a long, spreading puddle to an Estate gate. Here and there, across the windswept landscape, abandoned crofts lay in ruin and, still some distance away, an old stone cottage peeped flirtatiously through a clutch of bare trees. Corrunich. The old, stone cottage we had come to see. A green door and two big windows. To our eyes, it looked enchanting. Set in open moorland, 1,500 feet above sea level, with hills rising steeply behind, it was indeed remote. And having thoroughly examined the relevant OS map, we already knew that the surrounding hills led into more hills and, beyond those, more. A wilderness in miniature.

'I hope it's not too small,' I said in a low voice as we approached the cottage. I wasn't talking to anyone in particular, just voicing my own fear. Small had been the repetitive characteristic of our search so far. Our requirements were simple or so we had thought. A small cottage with some land and outbuildings to convert. In a remote spot. You wouldn't think that would be difficult in the highlands but, for two long years, the right property had eluded us. The cottages had either been too small with poky rooms and low ceilings or too small with too high a price and outbuildings beyond repair. At a glance, Corrunich looked no different. A tiny stone box. Sturdy, yes, but built for the weather, not the view. But, as we rounded the gable end into the open-armed embrace of the L-shaped barns, a bubble of excitement lodged, *whoomph*, in my chest. The barns, which formed the rudiments of a courtyard, were at least twice the size of the cottage. And, from the back, the cottage gave the illusion of being taller. We all tumbled out of the vehicle and took in the view. Breathtaking, open space. I knew this was it. I could feel it. Not yet immune to disappointment though, I tried to suppress my surging excitement just in case any horrors lurked within.

We entered the cottage through what would once have been the lean-to milk house, part of which had been converted into a small back porch. Not big enough to swing a cat in but slightly larger than a telephone box. Enough room for dirty boots and a few wet jackets. The remaining section of the milk house formed a primitive kitchen area, no more than a sink and a work surface, which opened up into a larger, stone-floored room in which the sole features consisted of an old solid-fuel stove set in the original fireplace and wooden wall panelling, stained dark brown. I could picture our old pine kitchen table, stripped and restored by my father, set in the middle of the room with our reconditioned whisky barrels for storage and possibly an old rocking chair in the corner to the side of the stove. There would be little space for anything else but it would be cosy.

Two doors led off that room. One to a good-sized, wooden-floored bathroom which, in the days before the recent indoor plumbing, had been a downstairs bedroom with an open fireplace. The stone hearth now proudly supported a gleaming white loo. The other door led into the main narrow hall where the front door, the green one we had seen from the track, was located and off which the rest of the cottage flowed. On the far side of the hall a door opened into the sitting-room, the one room that needed attention right away. It reeked of damp and mould, the source of which was seeping through the plaster on the south-facing gable end. By lifting up the edges of the mangy, beige carpeting which was soaked in parts, we could see that some of the underlying floorboards were rotten. And the tiny fireplace set into the soggy, sponge-like wall looked as if it would have about as much effect as a lit match in a breeze. But, with the enthusiasm of new campers, we focused on the bright side. By ripping out the carpet and tearing down the plaster we might even uncover a handsome stone wall with a huge fireplace.

Back into the hall and up the smooth wooden stairs, flanked by heavy cast-iron railings, and on to the narrow wooden landing with a bedroom at either end. With sloping ceilings and skylight windows, both were bright and, for this type of cottage, surprisingly spacious. Big enough for a double bed and a set of drawers and high enough for a six-foot guest. One we would sleep in, the other we would use as a temporary office. And, between the two bedrooms, lay the jewel in the crown. A tiny loo, created by building a dormer window out from the roof, with the best view of the hills. As I took a second look around all the rooms, I was practically squeaking. Excited squeaks. As if I had sucked balloons. It was all so perfect. And wonderfully basic. No central heating, no mains electricity and no phone but plenty of fresh water running straight off the hill. The post-box was over a mile away at the bottom of the track, the nearest phone box was about two miles away, and the nearest village, Tomintoul, was ten miles away. To two people who, for the last ten years or so, had lived in busy cities, the whole set-up sung of liberation. Basic and remote. Solitude and challenge. Just what we were looking for. Mentally, I had already moved in. The old cottage was just begging to be lived in and cared for like a dear old lady.

The potential of the barns lay beyond our expectations. They had once housed a cow byre, turnip shed, stable area and hayloft and seemed to be in remarkably good condition. Alan and Dalla, the two English lads who owned the property, had even scraped out all the old manure which now lay in a heap beyond the boundary fence. Later in the year, they sent us a set of early architectural drawings of the property. Beautifully executed on parchment paper, they detailed the repairs to the dwelling house in 1910, the construction of the barn and turnip shed in 1915, and the addition of an adjoining barn and stable in 1916. It was interesting to see how little had changed since the property, then titled Corrunick, belonged to a P. McPherson. It was a tangible record, worthy of framing, if it hadn't been for the crude red and blue biro lines scribbled around the drawings – Alan and Dalla's route plan for the installation of the indoor plumbing and drainage.

The roomy barns still revealed evidence of their former uses. Dried cow dung clung to the walls and posts; old wooden stable partitions smoothed by the continual rubbing of ponies' heads and rumps; long hooks and shredded harnesses; the remnants of straw and grain caught between the cobbles on the ground; huge, square,

shuttered windows for tossing in the hay; a small peep
hole in the corner that once held the shaft of a water-
wheel; a rickety, rotten, shit-smeared ladder that led up to
the watertight hayloft; the nests and droppings of numerous rabbits, bats and pigeons. And, through it all, we
could envisage the beginnings of our dream: the creation
of photography workshops.

We both loved photography. All aspects of it, but particularly black and white. Jonathan had studied the art
with a leading Cuban photographer in America. I was less
trained, with successive reels of unpredictable film, but
deeply interested. So we saw the workshops as a way of
immersing ourselves in something we loved and, at the
same time, giving ourselves the opportunity to learn and
improve. To keep things simple and to keep the cost
down, we would start with black-and-white photography
workshops. That meant drawing up plans for a spacious
studio, dark-room and work area. Any colour work that
we might take on would be processed at professional labs.
We felt quite confident that Jonathan would be able to
teach the basic workshops but we also intended to bring in
specialist photographers for the advanced ones. And,
given the space in the barns, we would have room to
house these specialist photographers while those taking
part in the workshops would be found accommodation in
Tomintoul. In our minds, it all seemed so clear and exciting. We were modelling the workshops on successful ones
in America so the only foreseeable problem was the cost.
Not the cost of organising and running the workshops

but the cost of converting the barns. Funds for that would have to come from the bank or the local Enterprise Trust, which meant putting together a watertight business plan. Fortunately, with the sale of our New Town flat in Edinburgh, we had the money to buy the property outright and enough money left over to live off for a year. Plenty of time to research the workshops, get other photographers on board, and put together the business plan.

'So are you going to go for it?' asked Liz, sidling up to us as we stepped out of the barns into the clean air.

'Yes,' we both replied, without a moment's hesitation.

'Good,' our sage friend continued. 'Because even if it doesn't work out, you'll never forget living here.'

I stood quietly in the garden and drank in the feeling of space. That liberating feeling of space that makes me feel good to be alive. Not flat, blank space but engaging views with depth. Views that stretch into the distance and lure me into deep reverie. And the view that stretched before me was open and relaxing. Calming. A view I could get lost in for hours. An isolated glen framed by voluptuous hills.

It often strikes me how the experiences you have as a child can shape you for the rest of your life. My early childhood was in Africa and my teenage years in the Scottish highlands so I tend to draw my breath from wide open spaces and the untamed landscape. My best childhood memories are of my brother and I running around freely in endless space. We had five acres of garden filled with the colours and scents of frangipani, bougainvillaea, jacaranda, poinsettia, and arum lilies. We fired our airguns and collected snakes. We climbed for loquats and crawled down ant-eater holes. We watched the chameleons change colour and we used long grasses to tickle baboon spiders out of their holes. We ate pawpaws and mangoes for breakfast and drank gallons of passion-fruit juice. We swam and snorkelled in the warm Indian Ocean and played in the pearl-white sand under the palm trees. We rode horses over the plains and through forests that concealed leopard and we camped in the bush listening to the wild animals around our tent. In fact, the only memorable crack in my idyllic childhood came when my parents moved from East Africa to Glasgow. Nowhere could have been more different. Immediately, I felt squeezed by the drab buildings and damp air. The atmosphere was enclosed. There was a familiar smell of curry powder on Gibson Street and there were black faces on the buses but that wasn't enough for me. I felt utterly confined. The fact is I was never there for very long and may have grown to like it if I had stayed but, as my fascinating, albeit inadequate, schooling in Africa had rendered me behind the Scottish standards, I was sent off to a boarding-school that would enable me to catch up. And there, of course, I really was confined. Instead of watching the baboons rubbing their blue bums against our classroom windows, or shooing the zebra and giraffe off the pitch so we could play hockey, I found myself behind high walls with the freezing North Sea wind blowing straight up my little gym skirt. Aside from the chapped legs and numb fingers, I soon got accustomed to it but there did, however, linger a touch of melancholy which, invariably, raised its head in paintings and stories. Somehow, I turned everything into Africa. In a land where the animals are spotted and striped, where the insects and reptiles are more colourful than a rainbow, where the black nights echo with the sounds of chirping crickets, belching bullfrogs, and barking hyenas, and where the tone of skin and style of dress varies from tribe to tribe, how can you fail to be influenced? Even the soil is red. Some teachers marked my stories as too far-fetched. Or, deviating from the truth. It was most unfair. The stories were true. At least, they were a child's interpretation of the truth. But a child is unaware how trapped adults become by their own limited experiences.

My parents, however, were aware that after living in Africa our lives had changed. We all needed space. So they bought a holiday cottage just out of the village of Braemar. Nothing could replace our memories of Africa, experiences like that remain with you for life, but the chill, fresh air of the purple hills became my cure and, although my parents were based in Glasgow, I promptly regarded Braemar as my home. Simply because of that feeling of space. Later, when I left university, I continued to search for that feeling of space, never quite at peace until I had found it. In the cities of Italy, Turkey, and America, I tried to find apartments with a balcony and a view and when the weekend approached, I would pack my bags and drive into the country or to the coast. In Istanbul I reached the pinnacle of my search for a room with a view. My office, which was situated at the very top of an old, tall building and was reached by an ancient, creaky, caged elevator, had a spectacular view along the Bosphorus and out to the Sea of Marmara, and over the Golden Horn to the Topkapı Palace. It was like sitting on a giant's throne, perched at the junction of Europe and Asia. I could rule the world from there. It was easy to see how the mighty Ottomans did. My office even had a balcony on which I and my Turkish colleague sipped gin and tonic, completely captivated by the movement of the busy boat traffic and lulled by the haunting sound of the call to prayer echoing from all sides of the water. It was such a fascinating view, I had to exercise a great deal of restraint to prevent myself from watching it all day long. In Istanbul I also met Jonathan. I didn't like him at first and he didn't like me. But somehow we became friends and embarked on midnight runs at the weekends, driving through the night into the heart of Anatolia, or high up into the lush mountains, or to a quiet place on the coast. It was like an adrenalin rush as our senses became alive in the open spaces. On Monday mornings we would be back at work. When seeking space and solitude, distances never pose a problem.

The more I thought about it the more it made sense for me to be in this part of the highlands. It would be a bit like coming full circle. My wanderlust had taken me on a circuitous route but now that I was ready to put down some roots and embark on new dreams, it had led me home. Even in my wildest dreams I had never imagined I would end up here. Before meeting Jonathan, I had been bound for South America but love wrecked all plans and I followed him to the States instead. And then we moved to Edinburgh where we made the decision that it was time to do our own thing in a place we wanted to be. And that place was the Scottish highlands. Because they were wild and fresh and there was no one there. It was just as exciting as going abroad and, for Jonathan, it was a completely new country. His whole life had been split between London and Istanbul. Everyone that knew him regarded him as a city man. His parents were city people and so one assumed he was too. But he was as keen to move here as I was. We were both longing to live in a remote spot. And that longing was probably born from his childhood experiences too. Certainly, his childhood was unique. He had the privilege to grow up in the largest *yalı* (Ottoman mansion house) on the Bosphorus. Built spectacularly with its foundations right in the water, it had clear views up and down a wide stretch of the Bosphorus and to the hills on the other side. His grandmother would lean out of the window and buy fish from passing boats and, as the tankers glided by, the waves splashed, with some force, right up against the windows of the salon and dining-room. Bought in 1840 by Jonathan's great-great-great grandfather, Kıbrıslı Mehmed Emın Paşa, who was appointed Grand Vizier of the Ottoman Empire in 1854, the *yalı* remains to this day in the hands of Jonathan's extended family. In Jonathan's grandmother's days, the *yalı* was regularly visited by European dignitaries, royalty, and well-known writers and artists, like Pierre Lotti. One of Jonathan's great uncles had been a distinguished writer, another had been the Ambassador to Cyprus, his grandfather had been a diplomat in Germany and Japan, and his great grandfather had been the Ambassador to Russia and Sweden, so languages and the finer points of culture were no strangers to the light and airy, high-ceilinged rooms with views over the water to one side and over the vast garden to the other. There were bamboo woods, an orchard, a vegetable garden, a hillside forest, a private beach and swimming area, servants and a milking cow. Boats were tied to the jetty in front of the tamed lawns and the sound of lapping waves, crickets, and frogs reverberated in the warm air. Although the Estate had been significantly reduced by the time Jonathan came along, it was still a child's paradise with seemingly never-ending space and stunning views. Hardly, I admit, a training ground for living in the wilds of the Scottish highlands, but there must have been something there. A kindled sense of adventure, perhaps? Or could it just have been that liberating feeling of space again?

As I stood with my feet firmly on highland soil, reflecting on what had set us on this trail, I was continually drawn into the view. One could easily be mistaken in thinking it was part of the property. There wasn't a lot of land with the property but the view was just there, on the other side of the fence. I could step into it, like Mary Poppins stepping into the painting. There were no roads to cross, no houses to pass, just open moor that led into the hills. They were by no means the most beautiful hills in the Scottish highlands. They didn't emit the stunning drama of the jagged peaks of the west highlands, but they were calmer to the eye. Perhaps, I thought naïvely, easier to live amongst. And infinitely more peaceful. For they were Corbetts rather than Munros, of no interest to the 'Munro bagger' and, therefore, less disturbed. Scarred with the ubiquitous, blotchy patches of burnt heather, they were grey and green, at different stages of rejuvenation. The hallmark of all grouse territory. It is almost as if some great, clumsy hand has stamped a map of the world across the hills, repeatedly featuring continents like India, Africa and South America. And through these continents snaked the continuation of the shooting track. Like an open wound. The only blot, so to speak, on the landscape. Easy vehicular access into the hills, and up them. John Hammond, the agent who was showing us the property, told us about his experience on a similar track on Ben Rinnes, the highest peak in the distance. With his other cap on, that of a shooting tenant, he had driven his Range Rover up it in winter and got stuck at the top. There was no way he could get the vehicle down so he got out his mobile phone and called a taxi. See you at the bottom in an hour, he had told the driver, before having to head down the hill on foot. I had to laugh. But I did wonder if anyone *walked* in the hills anymore.

Certainly, walking was what I had in mind. Every day if I could. There is something about the highland hills that, for me, surpasses all others. They feel so familiar. And I can walk in them freely. Alone. There are no herders that just happen to pop up when you're having a pee, no bandits waiting in the hidden glens, and no dangerous wild animals to worry about. I remember only too well how long it took my mother and I to shake off our fears of wild animals lying in the long grass when we returned from East Africa to Deeside. Out walking at dusk we might, inadvertently, disturb a roe deer grazing quietly behind a clump of juniper. Startled by our presence, it would jerk its head up and flee into the woods. Instinctively, we would jump with fright. Then we would feel rather silly and laugh at our ridiculous reaction. We were in the Scottish highlands not the African bush. Apart from the adder, which we had yet to encounter, the wildlife was generally shy and harmless. Not like the leopards that had prowled our garden at night, the hyenas that had circled our camps, or the angry buffalo that had once charged us in a forest. That particular buffalo had been rather too close for comfort. You would think that in a forest the logical route to safety would have been to climb a tree but, to our horror, the tall trunks were smooth and narrow, only sprouting into branches and foliage at the very top. There was nothing within reach to grip on to. So as the buffalo, with its deadly horns, bore down upon us, we dived behind a solitary bush and held our breath as the ground shuddered under the heavy buffalo's hooves thundering right past us on the tail of the dogs.

Back in Edinburgh, seated comfortably in his plush, over-heated, airless office, our lawyer advised us against buying the cottage. The surveyor's report had not been favourable. We would be paying too much for a pile of stones in the hills. He glanced at the report and laughed nervously, distractedly picking at the spots on his face. The cottage was remote, it had limited access, there were no locks on the windows, no security system, no phone. What about insurance, he wailed.

Understandably, our lawyer and friends thought we were mad. Why on earth do you want to live in the highlands? they asked. It's a place for holidays, not one's home. We wouldn't fit in. We had lived in vast, vibrant cities like Istanbul and New York. We were interested in photography, travel and food. Jonathan dreamed of owning a vineyard and, ever since I was a child, I had dreamed of working with elephants. So why the highlands? The rain, the mist, the midges? The long, bone-chilling winters? The short, unpredictable summers? The uncertainty of coping? The risk of losing? We would be turning our backs on comfortable living, with only an idea for a business and little wherewithal to do it. Why didn't we move to the Mediterranean? To the sun, sea, garlic and olives? That would have made sense.

It is true that if you're not born in the highlands, it's a difficult place to penetrate. It is resistant to change. Most young people with any sense have left. There's nothing there for them to do. A consuming emptiness stretches between farms and villages and between villages and towns. More windswept moor than sheltering trees. More sheep than people. More wariness than welcoming. And we had chosen to leap into its very depths to buy a remote property in an isolated glen. But, to us, that all sounded very appealing. We didn't really question our motives. We didn't even look too far ahead. It was just instinctive. There are only a few moments in one's life that present themselves for the taking, and this was one of them. We had to grab it by the balls as we might not get the chance again. If we wanted to actually live some of our dreams, we knew we had to create the circumstances ourselves. The photography workshops were only the beginning and, with a little luck, they might lead on to other things. More travel, perhaps? The production of books and documentary films? Those elephants and the vineyard? There's nothing wrong with dreaming and we had absolutely no idea how difficult it all would be.

Besides, the answers didn't lie in Edinburgh either. Our biggest fear was to be shackled by the monotonous security of jobs devoid of soul. We could waste our lives doing that. I already felt that I had just wasted two years in a low-paid job with a bunch of middle-aged men who bickered relentlessly and wore mediocrity like a comfortable old coat. Stowed away, in spite of my supposed prominent position within the company, in a damp, dirty basement office without a window or any ventilation. And added to my chagrin, I had had to share the squalid basement with a heavy smoker and the frequently used, odorous toilet where mould grew with a vengeance and flies stuck to the wet walls. The conditions were worse than Brixton Prison, remarked one visitor who was well acquainted with that establishment. Having worked and travelled in a number of countries, some of them desperately poor, I hadn't expected such squalor and apathy in Scotland's capital city and I could feel that the depressing, stagnant atmosphere was sucking in every ounce of my erstwhile vitality. It was as if I had lost sight of the girl who had once been the junior swimming champion of Kenya, a teenage cross-country runner, and a twenty-something ski instructor. The athletic spring that had once been in my step had slid disgracefully into a slothful waddle and I was metamorphosing into a thirty-something marshmallow instead. It was time to push myself again. To bound over the hilltops, like a free spirit, with the wind in my ears. To regain that supreme feeling of being physically and mentally alert. So, for the sake of my sanity, if nothing else, I needed to be decanted.

While we packed up and emptied our flat, Biglie sat huddled in a corner with his ears drooping, the picture of misery. Dogs don't like change at the best of times, but we were convinced he thought he was going to be sent back to the Edinburgh Cat & Dog Home where we had got him at six weeks old. Abandoned with his siblings, some black, some golden, he had seemed the cheekiest and sturdiest, tumbling over the others, proudly displaying the white patch on his chest. We didn't quite know what breed he was, possibly an Alsation/Retriever cross, but, given the length of his whiskers he was sure to grow into something big, so we had named him accordingly. And he had come cheap – £30.00 and a bag of puppy food. He had been my thirtieth birthday present and I was smitten. Even when during the night, missing the warmth of his siblings, he would climb on to my pillow and curl into my hair. A habit that I was loathe to discourage as I felt he needed all the comforting he could get. But it was a habit that never failed to wake me up with the sensation that I was wearing a fur hat in bed and then continued to deprive me of sleep as I anticipated an unwelcome baptism in the form of a warm trickle around my ears.

Wherever we went Biglie came too but on the few occasions we had to leave him alone, he would dash around the flat in defiance looking for something to attack. We couldn't resist lingering for a minute or two on the other side of the door, sneaking a peep at him through the letterbox. Usually he'd grab the yellow washing-up gloves dangling over the kitchen sink and race around shaking them like a rat. But on one occasion his bout of defiance got him into trouble. We returned to find him sitting triumphantly on the bed with his spoils – Jonathan's Spanish cowboy boots. Worn and waxed for years, these travelled boots had seemed indestructible until Biglie's needle-sharp puppy teeth had successfully chewed a spiky chunk out of one of them.

Once we were on the move, Biglie began to cheer up. The three of us left Edinburgh and headed north in our compact car, stuffed to bursting with sacks of bread flour, spices, bottles of pungent olive oil, a doorstop block of Parmesan, bags of dark-roasted coffee beans, cases of wine and bottles of cask strength malt whisky. Our survival kit for the culinary desert that lay ahead of us. A Spanish couple touring the highlands had once asked us: 'What is this scampi? Every night we have scampi and chips, scampi and peas, scampi and beans. Is it a national dish?' Scampi had been on the menu throughout the highlands so, to ensure that we wouldn't ever have to dine on scampi, the aroma wafting around the car had us licking our lips in hunger instead. Even Biglie's tail was thumping, contentedly, against a supply of Sainsbury's gourmet dog food. Wriggling around on the back seat, he rested his head on a large sack of bread flour so that his nose poked through the gap between the front seats. Gently, I stroked the velvety fur at the end of his long, proud nose and told him about the wilderness he was going to have for a garden.

We stayed in a rented cottage while the lawyers sorted out the paperwork. But not for long. Knowing the time it can take lawyers, John Hammond, the agent, had already given us the keys to our new home. A relaxed arrangement.

Based on trust. We were in the country now, doing things the country way. There was no point rattling the nerves of our city lawyers with that one. The arrangement was that we could move in as soon as Alan and Dalla, the two English lads selling the property, had cleared out their belongings. They had come up from London for a few days to do just that so we thought it would be interesting to meet them.

As the track was still blocked with snow we walked out to the cottage in the peaceful morning light, the smell of peat fire smoke lingering in the air. Filthy, drab curtains were drawn across the downstairs' windows. No signs of life. The sound of our knock at the door seemed to jolt through the air like a gunshot but nobody stirred indoors. We decided to carry on walking and come back in a few hours. Half a mile further down the shooting track we peered in through the windows of Ladderfoot, the only other inhabited cottage in this remote spot. Similar in size and style, beside a burbling burn, it rested at the foot of the Ladder Hills. Hence its name. A weekend retreat, John had told us. Neighbours, but only part-time.

The lads were up stoking the Raeburn and making tea when we returned. One was long-haired and skinny, the other more athletic looking but neither fitted the outdoor image we had created in our minds. Alan, the thin one, grabbed Biglie by the chops, bopped him play-fully on the head and rubbed his ears. Always a good sign. We were invited in and sat around the table in the re-assuringly warm kitchen. Unexpectedly, two plump,

curly-haired girls tumbled into the room and weaved
around the table heading for the bathroom. They looked
like twins. Vaguely introducing us to their backs, Alan
pulled a small bag of grass out of his pocket and calmly
rolled a fat joint. Leaning back in his chair, enjoying the
first puff of his morning's intoxication, he watched Biglie
who was unabashedly giving his balls a noisy, vigorous
lick. Carefully and thoroughly executed. Lick, lick, lick.
Alan's fascination was so intense, the ash of his smoulder-
ing joint fell to the floor. He took another long,
thoughtful drag and with a satisfied sigh said in his slow
Cockney drawl: 'I'm glad I can't do that.'

Wearing steel-capped boots, Alan and Dalla had kicked
open the door to Corrunich and bought it. They had been
impressed by how remote and wild it was. Just what they
were looking for. Although it had been in a ruined state,
they had intended to do it up in a few months. Three
years later, it was still not finished. They had never spent
a whole winter in the cottage. In fact, they had never
really stayed in it for long periods of time. Because of
money. They had run out of it so often they had had to
return regularly to London to earn quick cash before carrying on with the renovations. Some things had come free
of charge though. The wooden panels lining the kitchen
walls had come out of a hotel in Tomintoul and the downstairs' wooden doors had been lifted, or should I say
appropriated, from a ruined cottage near the source of
the Livet. It had seemed like a good idea at the time.

Good doors left to rot. No one was using them. But as they staggered over the river and along the shooting track, bent over by the weight of each door, they both must have cursed their original enthusiasm. Two doors took two laborious trips, each trip lasting a full day. They had stopped regularly to rest, lying back in the heather with a joint, giggling at the prospect of being caught. The shooting tenant or ranger might come by. 'A door?' they would say, looking around them, bemused. 'Fuck me, so there is. Let's knock on it and see who's there.' But when they attempted to appropriate a water tank on the hill to supply Corrunich, their luck almost tripped them up. Just as they were about to hack away at the ground to remove the tank, a farmer passed by and pointed out that it already supplied the cottage and had done so for a number of years. They would in effect be stealing their own water supply. 'What a couple of plonkers,' they admitted good-humouredly, shaking their heads at the memory of all those frustrating days they had spent fetching water in gallon containers when, all this time, the water supply had been right under their noses.

'We're moving into Corrunich,' we said, pronouncing the word phonetically.

We were talking to the woman who had rented us the temporary lodgings – a roadside box, not much bigger than a large doll's house. She was a local woman and knew the cottages in the area. But she was looking at us with a vacant expression. As if we were speaking another language. Perhaps we were pronouncing it wrongly. We tried variations on emphasis. Still, we drew a blank.

'Aha,' she said, triumphantly, some time later. 'You're moving to Corwanak.'

'Corwanak?' we repeated, incredulously. Were we talking about the same place?

Her man knew it well, she assured us. But how does the lilting Corrunich become the coarse-sounding Corwanak? A map, dated to 1869, provided a possible answer. It showed the very same cottage under the title Corunak. And that, or at least a bastardised version of it, seemed to be what the locals called it. Intrigued, we called up our friend David Allison, the talented Scottish guitarist. He also worked as a journalist for Radio Scotland and agreed to ask some of his Gaelic speaking colleagues if they knew the meaning of Corrunich. 'There doesn't seem to be a direct translation,' he reported back. 'But, if you isolate the sounds, there is an approximation. Cor-un-ak means something like "open, barren place".' But some of the locals had other versions. Since 1774, the cottage had been known as Corwanich, place of rowans, or possibly peat, but no one was sure. As there was only one rowan and little peat in evidence, we adopted the translation David Allison had given us because, over two hundred years later, it described it perfectly.

Settling In

On the day we moved in, the highlands welcomed us in true spirit. Fierce winds, a bit of stinging rain, a bit of slushy snow, the sun bursting through the gaps in the clouds as they catapulted across the sky and round it went again, sometimes teasing us with a change of sequence but all the time reminding us that this was just a taste of what was to come. It was the middle of April. The hilltops, crusted with a fresh fall of snow, looked like giant iced buns. Flashes of light flicked across the slopes, altering the mood in seconds. We set up our trusty camp-cooker in the empty kitchen and made some coffee which we drank outside. Just because we could. The fists of bitterly cold wind pummelled our bodies but the coffee smelled and tasted so fine.

Biglie bounced around the garden Tigger-like, ears flapping wildly with each gust, his tail wagging erratically like a haywire metronome. Even the wind blowing up his bum seemed to tickle him with pleasure. This was heaven for a dog. He trotted around busily, sniffing the ground and cocking his leg on the tough clumps of long grass and overgrown weeds. And when nature called upon us, we joined him. The icy wind breezed around our exposed regions, murderously turning them blue. Unless you can pee at liberty in your own garden, some people say, you don't really live in the country. If that's the definition of secluded rural life, we had made it.

The removal lorry took ages to arrive. While we waited, I set about cleaning the cottage with an old worn brush and pan. From the trails of tiny black droppings, it was obvious that the mice had been at liberty to roam indoors but so had two jackdaws which seemed to be using one of the chimneys as a nest and, when I went upstairs to clean the bedrooms, I met them. Face to face. Some time later, after a great deal of vocal coaxing and the odd shake of the broom, the jackdaws reluctantly vacated the premises through the opened windows. Meanwhile Jonathan collected sticks from the woods and chopped some wood for the solid-fuel Raeburn to get some warmth into the cottage. And, in that time, the weather changed dramatically for the worse. The sky grew dark and the biting wind flung stinging sleet at right angles. At last, through the spreading mist, a huge lorry appeared on the brow of the hill and hesitantly steered through the big puddle and narrow gates. 'What do you want to live here for?' the driver asked grumpily as he and his mate jumped out of the cab. Coming over the Lecht Pass, the clutch had almost burnt out and when he had seen the state of the track he had thought someone must be winding him up. Now the force of the wind was practically tipping the lorry over. And added to that, it was 'bloody freezing'. Hot tea and bacon sandwiches were gladly accepted but not the offer of waterproof jackets. No, these Edinburgh boys were going to freeze and get the job done so they could get out of this 'God-forsaken' place as quickly as possible.

The job done some hours later, the driver punched the lorry into reverse. It wouldn't move. In his fury he pumped heavily on the accelerator and the wheels spun. Slush and mud flew into the air. The lorry was well and truly stuck. Not a happy moment. There was little we could do but go in search of a farmer. It was the start of the lambing, a bad time to bother any farmer, but only the force of a tractor would be able to pull the lorry out. For a fee, a young farmer came in his tractor and towed the lorry right around the cottage so it was facing the gate. And, with no word of thanks, the lorry driver roared up the track. Civilisation beckoned with urgency.

As it drew dark that first evening, Jonathan started up the Lister generator. For such a big machine it made an incredibly gentle noise, the calming putt-putt of an outboard engine on a small boat. It immediately transposed us to Istanbul, listening to the rhythmical sound of boats chugging up and down the Bosphorus. We could be crossing the busy water from Europe to Asia; or sipping chilled vodka and cherry juice amongst the pink and purple hydrangeas in the waterfront garden of the *yalı*; or, better still, devouring plump, juicy mussels fried in beer batter in a restaurant built out into the water, the waves splashing up on to the deck whenever a Russian tanker went by. This of course made us hungry. Thoughts of Istanbul always do. So we placed a couple of aubergines directly on to the gas flame of the camp-cooker and, as they smoked and farted enthusiastically, we searched in our boxes for the thick-set yoghurt, lemon, garlic and olive oil to be mixed with the cooked aubergine flesh. Snug in our barren kitchen, while the biting highland wind whipped around the cottage, we toasted our new home by dipping chunks of bread into our favourite Turkish garlicky fix.

After a frenzied game of backgammon in candlelight, I ran a piping hot bath and sank into it. The water was distinctly blue. It ran straight off the hill through limestone which made it quite harsh on the skin but delicious to drink. It actually had a taste. I wallowed, blissfully, in the bath until I felt warm enough to leap between our cold sheets in the breezy bedroom that was mildly perfumed with droppings of jackdaw. As we cuddled up to keep warm, we looked up through the skylight window above our heads. The storm had died down and the moon had come out. The quality of light was magical, like looking at a fine print. Streamers of wispy cloud trundled elegantly past the window as if they were clearing the screen so that our eyes could feast on our very own slice of clear star-studded sky. It felt like we were being shown something secret. We could almost hear the wind saying 'shush, don't tell anyone' as it rocked the rowan and beech trees outside the window on the opposite side of the room. A calming sound like the gentle crashing of waves against the shore. We could have been sleeping out on a beach or on the deck of a boat. We were so far away from the life we had been leading.

The next morning as we were preparing for a breakfast of toast and marmalade, the gentle putt-putt of the generator cut out. The flywheel had come off and flown out through the barn door, severing any link with electricity and toast. And could have severed a head if either of us had been near. Possibly with a twinge of premonitory guilt, Alan and Dalla had thought to leave us the card of *the* Lister man who worked out of Aberdeen. So we drove to the phone box and bucked with surprise when he answered his mobile number on the first ring. He was just over in Mull, he said casually. He would take us in on his way home.

And sure enough he was with us by late afternoon. A small figure at the wheel of a long-wheel-based Isuzu Trooper which was so packed with boxes and generator parts there was barely enough room for him. As a repairer and installer of generators across the highlands and its distant outposts, he spends a lot of time in this vehicle. Just that day he had crossed from east to west and was now on his way back to the east coast for the night. With a shake of his experienced head he pronounced our inherited generator dead. He could get us a reconditioned one and install it for about eight thousand pounds. Having just bought the cottage with what we understood to be a functioning generator, we didn't have a spare eight thousand pounds and resigned ourselves to a spell without electricity. In a way, we welcomed the romance of it. Sitting at the kitchen table, illuminated by my father's old storm lantern with its gentle, companionable hiss and faint smell of kerosene, as the mist drew in cutting us off from the rest of the world.

Life without electricity was not difficult, just time-consuming. And we were no strangers to this way of living. In countries like Turkey, long periods without power are quite common. So the daily chores began. The floors were cleaned with a vigorous sweep of the broom and the clothes were washed by trudging them with our feet in the bath and then hung out on the line to dry. We had no fridge so we poured a little of our icy water into the bottom of a bucket to keep butter and milk cool and, for cooking, we had the double-ring camp-cooker which ran on bottled gas and the oven compartment in the stove. We had often stayed in places where the facilities were basic so we had become accustomed to being fairly self-sufficient. If you're a versatile cook you're halfway there and I had been cooking since I was child. My parents had sent me to a Saturday cookery class in Kenya and then, when I was seventeen, to the cordon bleu school in London. The cordon bleu diploma had come in handy when I notched up debts at university or when I needed to make money for travelling. Wealthy people liked catered dinner parties and the fishing/shooting brigade liked catered lodges where, more often than not, the kitchen conditions were big but basic. And out of nowhere, a five or seven course meal was expected to appear on the table in two hours. I would find five brace of unplucked grouse in the sink, blunt knives in the drawers and electrical appliances that didn't work. Worktop space would be minimal so I would have food on trays on the floor as I tried to prepare several dishes at once. The birds would burn, so they would end up *flambéed* which, on the spur of the moment, I declared was a Swedish tradition and, by the time the pudding course came around, I was so hot and flustered I would inevitably trip over one of my carefully placed floor trays and send the pudding flying. Those were the days that Jonathan now refers to as my 'skinning a dinosaur with a teaspoon years' which is what it felt like at times. But my interest in food really didn't hinge on fancy dishes and feeding the rich. I was much happier with simple, tasty, rustic Mediterranean food that oozed garlic and olive oil which could be mopped up with crusty bread and always went well with a bottle of red wine. The kind of food I could prepare on a camp-cooker in a basic kitchen. So the lack of electricity didn't affect our cooking. In fact, it barely affected our daily living at all. It meant that we had to eat meat and fish on the day we bought it, so that we virtually became vegetarian, and we shifted from fresh milk to UHT. And it meant that we wrote letters on an old, heavy Underwood typewriter that we had bought in a Salvation Army store in Ohio and it meant that we had to light candles to find our way to the loo at night. But the only thing we missed was music. We occasionally bought batteries for the radio but Chuck Berry, Miles Davis, Dennis Brown and the Stones gathered dust in a box.

In the mornings, I began to bake bread for breakfast. I would set up the dough the night before and leave it to prove overnight. Ready for a little kneading and a brief second rising in the morning. It was the most basic thing I could possibly do and, living in such isolation, I would feel a fraud if I didn't make some steps towards self-sufficiency. After all, we couldn't just pop around the corner to buy a loaf. While the dough rose, I laboriously ground dark-roasted coffee beans from exotic sounding places like Nicaragua, Guatemala, Malawi, Mysore, and Java by hand (although I would gladly have given my aching right arm for an electric grinder) and then stepped outside into the nippy highland air to drink a mug of the freshly percolated brew, its enticing aroma awakening the senses before the first delicious sip.

As if performing a ritual, I nearly always carried my mug of coffee up the hillside to sit on a stone overlooking Corrunich. Calm and content, tickling Biglie's ears. There was no rush. I even had time to watch a bulging black slug open its wide, gummy mouth and slowly, ever so slowly, devour a leaf. Taking its journey as it came. I had felt at home in many places but here, in this tranquil spot, I felt I actually belonged. Here with that black slug. It was as if the place spoke to me. The animated space, the chill, fresh air, the sharp smell of pine from the woods and the grass wet from the night's rain. A kaleidoscope of intangible things. Like coming home. Our home. If only in the heart and mind. For Corrunich was here long before us and will still be here when we are long gone. To the highland way of thinking, we just 'bide' here. The guardians of the moment.

The first month in our new home was like living in a dream. A spell of warm, sunny weather washed the slopes of snow and set us in a holiday spirit. We woke to the merry sound of oyster-catchers and curlews busily nesting in the marshes and tried to trace the haunting drum of snipe in flight. Apart from the heartening sounds of nature, the days and nights were so quiet we really could hear the silence. We walked into the hills, the fresh air painting colour on our cheeks. It was like a moonscape on the tops – flat stones, shallow rain-filled pools, spongy red-and-green moss, wind-cropped heather, and great chunks of peat bog bitten out of the surface. The hares, still in their white winter coats, darted through the maze of bogs which were delightfully springy under foot. Like walking on a firm mattress. And, bravely standing no higher than a thumb, sturdy bright-green shrubs poked out of the low-lying moss and heather. They looked like shoots of an alpine plant but were, in fact, trees. Fully grown. A type of spruce, permanently stunted by the Arctic weather in the hills.

In the chilly evenings, ridiculously seated on striped, collapsible beach chairs that blew over the second we got up, we cooked and ate outside wrapped in warm fleeces and woolly hats. The absurdity of it reminded us of similar evenings in New York when, no matter how cold it was, we had enjoyed a drink outside on the deck of our rented Long Island beach house while our American neighbours had turned up their central heating and trotted around indoors in their shorts. But, in the highlands, we had no heating so it was almost as cold inside as it was out. Besides, we were enjoying the living screen. Watching the ancient hills, rounded like mammoth bosoms, bronzed from the glow of the setting sun. We could see why pioneering Scots felt at home in parts of North America, Canada, India and Africa, settling in pockets that reflected their much-loved highlands. In the differing light our view could be many a place. A place of solitude. And when the moon rose above our heads and lit up the clear aubergine sky, we welcomed it like an old friend. It was so close we could almost touch it. 'You know,' I said, during one of our wine-induced philosophical moments, 'the astronomers are right. The moon really is our nearest neighbour.'

While still in holiday mode, my parents arrived to see our new home. They crawled down the track towards the gate. Two ageing, but youthful, people with a lifetime of security and success behind them. A lifetime of defined roles and purpose. My father's father, who died long before I was born, had been Professor of Divinity at Glasgow University, my father's uncle had been a High Court judge in Edinburgh, my father's brother had been the minister at Dornoch Cathedral, and my father, himself, had been

Professor of Medicine in Nairobi and in the latter years, before his retirement, a leading cardiologist. My mother, who was also a doctor, came from a ministerial background too and had, at one time, regarded an overdraft as breaking the law and a mortgage as something to be ashamed about. She still felt that we ought to settle down and have 'proper' jobs. After all, her friends' children did.

As they drove in through the gate, I could read her expression clearly. Oh no, she was thinking, what have they done now? How are they going to earn any money out here in this tiny cottage? Yet again, she was going to have to endure the unconventional wandering of her daughter who had, invariably, made her grip the edge of her seat. Why couldn't we just get on with life like other people? 'Oh,' my mother exclaimed with instant relief, as she threw open the car door in the nook of the barn. 'It's much bigger than I thought.' My father, taking a little longer to extract himself from his seatbelt, heaved himself out of the low-set car and told us, with quiet sincerity, what a lovely place we had found. I knew they would like it but, I feared, only as a place to spend one's holidays. Moving here to set up a business, on the other hand, was beyond their ken. They stood for a moment and looked at the view. It reminded them of East Africa. Taking them back to their whitewashed veranda looking out, over the tomato and beetroot coloured bougainvillaea, to the Ngong hills. And then curiosity got a grip of my mother and spun her towards our shabby back door.

There was nothing they didn't like. The cottage and the

barn, they agreed, were both so full of potential. My father tapped walls and inspected beams, suggesting ways of preserving, restoring and generally making do. He had, after all, some experience in this. He had made suspended canvas beds to fit into the back of a Land Rover, he had built my mother several kitchens, cut and fitted floor-to-ceiling bookshelves, hammered together a table using the legs of hospital beds, beaten a sheet of copper into a hood for the fireplace, converted old oil lamps, and made cushions and padding from old jumpers stuffed with the moulted hair of his dogs. Every bit of wood, rubber or metal had a use. And at eighty years of age, he was still fit and able to live in a country cottage that was often snowbound in winter. Determined to stay there, he had developed systems, drawn from methods used in China and Africa for carrying wood and heavy loads, to make it easier for himself. He so loved where he lived that he was reluctant to leave it for any period of time. So I got the feeling that, even if he and my mother couldn't quite grasp what we wanted to do and how we would go about it, they could at least understand why we wanted to live here. That was half the battle.

Euphoric, we gravitated towards a jolly lunch of moist smoked venison. Smoked at a local kiln and sliced finely, it is the tastiest smoked venison I have ever had. Tossed with roasted peppers, feta cheese, sweet, juicy melon, fresh basil leaves, olive oil and lemon juice, it was delicious. By the end, my mother was positively ecstatic. 'Do a Peter Mayle!' she cried, waving goodbye on her way out of the gate. 'Here?' I queried in jest. In a country with no food culture? Where the supermarket checkout girl asked me what an aubergine was, thought a red onion was a plum, and offered to change my selected bunch of sweet (I had already tasted one), ripened yellow grapes for the 'bonnier' green ones which were excruciatingly sour. But, I understood what she meant.

Two weeks later we could be found huddled around the Raeburn as, overnight, the warmth of spring came to an abrupt end with a fierce snow blizzard. We couldn't see out of the skylight windows as they were plastered with a thick layer of fresh snow. The morning birdsong was momentarily strangled until the few courageous survivors regained the strength to begin all over again. Everybody, but us, had been expecting this change in the weather. It happens every year we were told, the Gab o' May, the return of the winter landscape in the middle of May. There is a local saying 'Keep some hay for the Gab o' May'. But even so, the farmers spent the first morning walking the fields prodding the snow-drifts with sticks hoping that some newborn lambs had survived. Many hadn't. It was as if the laughter of spring had become enveloped in a shroud of sadness. From that moment on we watched the weather with a new fascination. We were beginning to learn that, in the country, it really can make a difference to one's day.

There was still snow on the ground when we had our first argument. I have no idea what it was about, something trivial no doubt. I'm right and you're wrong, that kind of thing. But it drove Jonathan into such a fit of frustration that he stripped off all his clothes in the kitchen and ran out into the garden in just his socks As soon as his feet sank into the freezing snow, his naked body jerked, involuntarily, into a yelping, knee-kicking dance. Instantly, his temper dissolved and he whooped around the garden. With a beard and uncut, curly hair, it wasn't the first time he had resembled Billy Connolly. It was such a comical sight, I burst out laughing but I couldn't fully relax until I had scanned the empty horizon to see if anyone was watching. The trees and hills stared back. This was not a public display, nothing to be embarrassed about. I was just a captive of my own nationality. Forever bashful. I looked back at my husband, now cockily stamping out an improvised jig, Biglie barking and jumping around him, and marvelled at his lack of inhibition.

When Willie arrived at the back of eight, we were still in bed. We sprung into some clothes and attempted to greet him as if we had been up for hours. He had told us he would come at the back of eight which we thought might mean *after* eight but, evidently to Willie, it meant quarter to. He had come to clean the chimneys which were still stuffed with the twigs, leaves and feathers of the nesting jackdaws. With great intentions, we had bought a roof ladder but when it came to actually climbing up the ladder and balancing on the roof, neither of us had felt safe so we decided to watch someone else do it first.

We had knocked on the door of the only person we knew in Tomintoul. A fit Englishman who, in one of life's coincidences, we had sat next to on a plane returning from a ski holiday that winter. He had adopted Tomintoul as his home to be closer to the ski slopes and all the Munros he was in the process of bagging. And he had suggested we look for a cottage in the area. So here we were, a few months later, knocking on his door. He remembered us and after a friendly welcome of coffee and a Tomintoul dram, he had introduced us to Willie, a still-man by trade, who also does odd jobs like gardening, fencing and cleaning chimneys.

'Caught you with your pants doon, Je,' Willie teased. For some reason, only known to Willie, he called Jonathan, Je, pronouncing it like the French first person singular. Perhaps he couldn't remember Jonathan's name but was confident it began with J.

'Hope you didn't go buying this yourself, Je,' he said, inspecting our new, tinny-looking ladder. The words came out in a rapid burst, like the rata-tat-tat of a machine gun. Moulded in a thick accent, they were difficult to understand.

'Well, it's one thing buying it, and another using it,' Jonathan admitted sheepishly. Contrary to his earlier decision to say he had borrowed it.

'I'll stick with my own,' Willie laughed. 'It's nae too far to fall, but I'm buggered if I'm going to break a leg today.'

Then he caught sight of a skimpy brush perched on the end of a metal stem. It had been tagged in the shop for some fireplace function but next to Willie's bristly, well-used brushes it looked like something a dapper City gentleman would use on his suit.

'Did you make this, Je?' Willie asked politely, picking it up and turning it over in his hands.

'Ah, no,' Jonathan replied, hesitatingly. 'I bought it.'

Willie's laughter rippled and spluttered from wheezy lungs. Shaking his head in amazement, he walked over to his trailer and lifted out a short, narrow, home-made ladder. On the end he had fixed a set of pram wheels to roll the ladder up and down the roof slates. It looked steady and practical. The only thing he didn't have was a mirror. He looked at us expectantly. Surely, with a woman in the house we had a mirror. We did. But it was only the size of a small matchbox. Would that do?

'Aye, as long as I can see up the chimney with it.' He shook his head again. As if we were a puzzling breed.

Soon Willie was straddled over the ridge of the roof plunging his brushes into the chimney, the twigs and feathers tumbling into the fireplaces. I was in the kitchen making coffee when Jonathan burst in through the door saying he was to light the Raeburn. Suddenly Willie's voice, Tarzan-like, boomed down the chimney into the kitchen. We looked at each other blankly. Neither of us had any idea what he had just said. Amplified by the hollow chimney, another garbled outburst boomed into the kitchen. A maze of profanities. I caught a few of them.

'I think you've singed his bloody whiskers, Je,' I giggled.

A black-faced Willie came to the back door. It was a hand, he had wanted, not a fire. His stern expression broke into a beaming grin, his bloodshot green eyes shining like polished marbles. Aye, he'd have coffee and a dram. He needed both. He wasn't going to change his accent for anyone, he explained as he downed his dram. Instead, incomers should try to understand him. He was quite right and I felt a little ashamed. Here I was in my own country, the country of my birth, but I couldn't understand the man in it. Willie's dialect was from Aberdeenshire and that was difficult enough. But the Glenlivet vernacular was different again. At times I felt so lost, I could have been in the midst of tribal tongues. It amazed me that, in my own part of the world, I could be so out of my depth and often found myself smiling or nodding to I have no idea what.

The high-pitched bleating of lambs searching for their mothers disturbed those last snatches of early morning sleep. If you close your eyes and isolate the sound it is just like a baby's cry. A sound impossible to ignore. All of a sudden, we were surrounded. The open land around us had been transformed into a maternity field replete with the noise of sheep chewing and burping while the lambs leapt about playfully butting one another in between violent tugs at their mothers' teats. At first it was quite interesting. Like being on a farm without all the work that goes into running one. But then they started coming in through our gate and loose fences, shitting all over the garden. And one night two ewes fell down a deep pit that had been dug by Alan and Dalla in the corner of the garden.

Biglie discovered the trapped ewes in the morning and stood over the hole, barking. Fortunately, that was all he did. Taking a firm hold of Biglie, Jonathan and I drew straws. Who was going to rescue the petrified girls? Reluctantly, I lowered myself into the pit and tried to calm them, their explosive rear-ends smeared in shit, before heaving them out. I was surprised at how light they were. Like bags of air, covered in straggly wool, that wriggled awkwardly in my arms. Clinging to a straining Biglie, we herded them out of the garden and closed the gate behind their wiggling backsides as they trotted off, a little shaken but not stirred, to join the others.

It was time to train Biglie. To stop him tucking into the tempting morsels of shit and to teach him never to chase the sheep. Never. Farmers don't hesitate to shoot dogs chasing their sheep. They know them all individually. After several beatings he got the message but, even now, when he comes across them his ears go back, his tail goes down and he slinks past them, hen-toed, guiltily trying to conceal that he is, in fact, thinking about it.

And then we met our neighbours. It was inevitable but we had been dreading it. We had psyched ourselves up to expect the worst. They could be pompous and narrow-minded. Or nosy and interfering. So we hadn't been in a rush to meet them. But, one evening, when we were out walking Biglie near Ladderfoot we were spotted. A tall, white-haired gentleman dressed in tweed plus-twos, knee-length socks and a cap gave us a wave and strode out to meet us. His attire bespoke gentleman farmer or landowner, a member of the shooting fraternity, and, as it turned out, he was all of those but his boyish smile and open manner contradicted the inherent pomposity that one often encounters with such figures. Fishing a chilled bottle of tonic out of the stream, Hamish White, our part-time neighbour, invited us in for a drink. Pam, his wife, met us at the back door dressed in mossy greens, the smart but comfortable look of a country lady. Sparkling with warmth and grace she took us into the stone-floored kitchen warmed by a raging wood fire set in the original hearth. We sat on khaki canvas chairs drinking mildly chilled gin and tonic. Apologising for the lack of ice and the plastic cups, they explained that they hadn't begun to bring their belongings from home. Home was a large farm near Forres, Ladderfoot was their retreat. It was lovely to get away and listen to the sound of the birds, they said, and proceeded to give us a spontaneous rendition of the bird noises they knew. They had seen wild duck, curlews, greenshank, oyster-catchers, lapwings, snipe, ring-ouzels, falcons and heron. And, occasionally, they had caught sight of the dottrel and golden eagles that nest high in the hills. Wobbly after too much gin, we meandered the half mile home in a beatific trance. Our neighbours were charming, warm and friendly. We were so lucky. If they had been awful, life in our isolated glen could have been hell.

Shan stepped off the plane at Inverness in an Armani suit with a toothbrush in his pocket. That was his entire luggage. Tall, snappily dressed, with copper-toned Indian skin, he looked a little out of place in the land of welly boots and pink and white faces. We had reminded him that the cottage was pretty basic and the weather a great deal chillier than London, but being a busy property developer, he didn't own any clothes fit for the country. Besides, he was only staying for one night. He was our first visitor and it was fitting that it should be him. He was Jonathan's oldest and closest friend and it was he who had seen the cottage in the *Exchange & Mart*. When we had first told him that we had actually bought the cottage but that it had no phone or electricity he had laughed and said: 'Man, if that's what you wanted, I could have got you a cheaper place in the heat of India.'

The sun was out so we insisted on sitting outside. We wrapped him up in a warm jacket and tucked his Armani bottoms into a pair of rubber boots. Wherever the sun shone, we sat. Sunny days in Scotland should be worshipped outdoors, we explained. Days to be enjoyed with a bottle of wine, garlicky dips, pickled hot peppers, and slices of locally smoked wild salmon. Just what we were doing when John Stuart, the farmer who tenants the fields around us, rode by on his quad with a gun slung over his shoulder and stared straight at us. We hadn't met him yet so we waved cheerfully, perhaps too cheerfully. He didn't wave back but rode close to our fence without averting his stare. Letting us know he's been here a lot longer than us, we assumed. Marking his territory. The primeval habit common to man and beast. 'Or he's never seen anyone so suntanned in the Braes,' joked Shan.

'So, is your *faether* a Turkey?' Norman Stuart barked through loose, blackened teeth and the well-sucked pipe firmly planted in the depths of his grizzly beard and moustache.

This was the first time we had met this big bear of a man. It was he who farmed the land below the shooting track. A forlorn outpost in the deserted glen. His sheep wandered and grazed in the hills but his cows were fed at the top of the field by the track. Most evenings, before we could see it, we would hear his old blue tractor spluttering up the hill, followed by the faithful line of cows. A burly figure would jump out of the cab and spread the hay before strolling over, with a crook hooked over the bend in his arm, to the gate at the corner of the field. There he would leisurely smoke his pipe and, under the pretext of looking to the hills beyond our cottage, he would watch us. Outwardly, he appeared rough with baggy, muck-smeared clothes hanging around his well-fed tummy but his bloodshot, blue eyes exuded warmth. An earthy Pavarotti with a boom in his voice to match.

'Yes, he's Turkish,' replied Jonathan, quick off the mark.

'My mother's English and I'm somewhere in between.'

'Ah, aye,' nodded Norman, the pipe smoke circling his weather-beaten face. You could see him digesting this fact. It made sense. That's why Jonathan spoke English with no trace of an accent. 'Best to keep the English part to yourself,' he added with a smile.

'I'm Scottish,' I proffered merrily. 'I spent my childhood in East Africa so I don't have a Scottish accent,' I explained, almost apologetically. And added that my father has a tape of me, aged three, singing *skinny milinky long legs and big banana feet* in a Scottish accent. I was beginning to feel the need to confirm my nationality. Highlanders have a way of staring right through you. They seem to need convincing. But Norman, whose face was almost obscured by the pipe smoke, made no comment.

'So, have you farmed here all your life?' I asked, changing tack.

'Aye, born in that house,' he replied, jerking his head in the direction of the tired-looking cottage somewhere over the hill.

'Does that mean you're related to the other Stuarts in the Braes?' I pursued. The Braes seemed to be made up of three families and the Stuarts were one of them.

'Distant.' He drew heavily on his pipe.

'So are you a cousin of John Stuart?'

'John *Belnoe*?' he asked in a delightfully vague way, as if he wasn't sure who we were talking about. There was no other John Stuart in the Braes. As the locals identified one another by the name of their farms or cottages, he was known as Belnoe, the name of his farm. We had joined the ranks as the 'Corwanaks'.

'Very distant,' he mused. He removed the pipe from his mouth and his eyes fixed on a point in the distance. He seemed to be thinking.

'There was a Stuart relative at Ladderfoot,' he added, as if this was suddenly a revelation. 'A distant aunt through marriage. Her man was killed in Aberdeen. Crossing the road and got knocked down by a car. I wouldn't blame the driver, though,' he chuckled, entertained by the memory. 'He was a man that liked a good dram and forgot he was in the city.'

On Midsummer's Evening, I sat outside and read a book. The light barely faded. I could see the page clearly, as if it was daylight. The sun had set earlier but the light had remained. Around midnight, it dimmed a little but it never got dark. I could have read outside all night as the sun was due to rise again in a few hours. According to the locals, that was when our summer would begin. Midsummer on the calendar but the beginning of summer in the high-lands. Time to plant and grow. And, as we were about to discover, midsummer also marked the beginning of the shooting. In the evenings, sometimes early, sometimes late. During the new hour of darkness, between midnight and one. The searchlight on top of the vehicle shone its powerful beam around the cottage and through the windows. Biglie barked and we all got up. Damn poachers, we cursed. Or keepers. Whoever it was obviously had no consideration for our sleep. And why, with all this space around us, did they have to shine their infernal beam at us? And shoot? This was the kind of thing you were unaware of when you bought a property in the country. But, we realised, we couldn't have escaped it in the highlands. We had wanted to live remote and, unless you are a landowner, that usually means on a hill farm or a shooting estate. Corrunich was on both.

As the summer progressed, I found myself rapidly becoming more and more territorial. Four-wheel drive vehicles were coming and going along the track and we had no idea who they were. One morning a short-wheel-based Toyota had come at us so fast, we had had to pull off the track to let it go by. The driver hadn't stopped or waved. He didn't look like a keeper, farmer or shooting tenant so we had jumped to rash conclusions and sped back to the cottage. We hadn't been away long, only to the village and back but, having adopted casual country habits, we had left our back door open. And there, jammed into the space where the bottom of the door didn't quite meet the stone floor, flapped a wad of colourful pamphlets. Jehovah's antennae had located us with lightning speed. All the way out here in our splendid isolation. A most unexpected intrusion.

So when a Land Rover pulled up in the field below our cottage I couldn't contain my curiosity and strolled over to see who it was. Not knowing what I was going to say, I tried to appear casual, as if I always took a walk in the field at that hour. Just as I reached the back of the vehicle, a gun poked out of the window on the driver's side, followed by the tips of a pair of binoculars and a glimpse of cropped fair hair. There was no turning back now so I strode right up to the window.

'Hi,' I said, in as bold a voice as I could muster. 'I've just come over to introduce myself.' I felt silly. Here I was accosting a man with a gun in the middle of a field and he was behaving as if he hadn't heard me. Without a doubt, I was a pest. I cleared my throat, self-consciously.

'We've come to live at Corrunich and have no idea who anyone is so I thought I would come over and say hello,' I blurted to the back of his motionless head.

Steadily the binoculars lowered to reveal a stern, but pleasant, face reddened with weather. It broke into a slow, bemused smile. His name was Sandy, the keeper for the hills around us. He was softly-spoken and calm, almost gentle, as he patted the head of an old, golden Lab lying on the floor of the passenger side. She had been his shooting dog but was too old now so she just accompanied him in the Land Rover.

'Are you looking for deer?' I asked, indicating to the binoculars and gun.

'Crows,' he said. 'They take the young grouse.'

'Tell me,' I ventured, addressing a subject that had concerned us. 'Do you know if the rotting stomachs lying in the marshes are poisoned?'

'No, they'll just be from the gralloching,' he said, matter-of-factly. That's when they slit open the belly of the dead beast, he explained, and remove the stomach and intestines so it's lighter to carry back to the vehicle.

'I've heard you rip out the liver and eat it while it's still warm?' It was the rituals of hunting that interested me.

'Some of the older keepers do,' he confirmed, screwing up his face in distaste.

'What about the shooting at night?' I broached. 'Is that you?' I knew I would feel better about it if it was.

'Probably the farmers,' he replied, shaking his head. 'Rabbits and hares. Shouldn't be anything else.' And gave me a wry look.

We were just about to tuck into a piping hot dish of *beğendi* when a gunshot, fired too close for comfort, made us jump. *Damn.* This food was too good to be disturbed in the middle of. A soothing mush of pulped smoked aubergine in a cheese sauce, which was usually served in Turkey as an accompaniment to meatballs, it had delighted one of the Ottoman Sultans and now our version, topped with grated Parmesan cheese, and browned in the oven and served with a green salad, was about to send us to celestial heights. But here was our chance to tackle who-ever had been shooting around our cottage at night. And we had decided I should be the one to do it as it might seem less aggressive coming from a woman.

With the *beğendi* back in the oven, I rushed outside with Biglie who shot out of the gate and pinned the shooting party to the hillside with his deep, fierce-sounding bark, keeping them in check with his flashing teeth. Nobody dared move. The light, draining from the sky, leant a sombre background to the scene. I recognised John Stuart, the tenant farmer, amongst the group of stony-faced men with their sons and guns. Grabbing Biglie by the scruff of his chunky neck, I tried to be friendly in the adverse circumstances. They had been shooting around the cottage for years, the fact that someone now lived in it, didn't seem to matter. This was the point I wanted to make. To their ears I must have sounded pompous but I was determined to stand my ground. Their faces were difficult to read as they stared right through me. They had seen people come and go in the glen. And I was just another one, who didn't understand the ways of the country. The only sign that my plea for courtesy had been heard came from John Stuart who gazed into the distance with steely eyes and sighed a long, drawn-out 'Oh, aye'.

'Well, well,' Norman greeted us gruffly at the gate. He was looking particularly rough and shaggy that day.

'We've been looking for illicit stills in the hills,' we told him. We had followed the route of whisky smugglers and their sturdy garrons, laden with kegs. A journey that took them eastwards over the hills from the Braes to the shores of the North Sea. And south to places like Brechin and Perth. We didn't go that far but kept our eyes open in the hills between the Braes and Strathdon, the first leg of the smugglers' journey.

'You'll be lucky to find one of those,' he chuckled knowingly around his pipe. All the locals had combed the hills.

'We can always live in hope,' Jonathan said, cherishing the thought. He does love his whisky.

'Aye, well they all used to make their own whisky around here,' Norman said wistfully. 'They say there's an exciseman buried in the peat bogs down there,' he added, pointing to the moor at Ladderfoot. 'Came over the hills from Strathdon to the door of one of the crofts. The man of the house was out on the hill with the beasts so he asked the wife for the money. Wait here, she said to the exciseman, I'll go inside and get it. She returned with a gun and shot him dead.'

A Land Rover pulled up outside our gate. It was the Estate ranger and his wife. Not a local ranger of the Yogi Bear variety but an Englishman geared to promoting the Estate. In theory there was nothing wrong with that but, on an Estate where the landowners (the Crown) are absentee and the factors speak in public-school tongues, the appointment of another Englishman must have been like a poke in the eye for the locals. And a conflict of interest. There was already a strain on the land with a Dutch shooting tenant, a team of local keepers, and generations of farming families, all of whom were on the land every day and regarded it as theirs. There was so little land to spare that even the ranger's wife, who had been given a grant to start up a highland pony centre, had nowhere to put the ponies. So she had arranged to use the open land around Corrunich. A temporary arrangement – thank God – as she planned to bring groups up to see the ponies. And the thought of people invading our sanctuary (as it felt like our very own) made my heart sink.

The ranger and his wife had come to clear the land of old bits of rusted barbed wire that had been left in the long grass and juniper bushes by previous tenant farmers. The sheep had managed to graze their way around the wire but cantering, playful foals might not. Keen to rid the land of this hazard, I offered to help, tugging and pulling at the tangled wire. Some of it was so firmly bedded in the soil, the ranger had to pull it out with his Land Rover. It was a common sight in the highlands – sharp wire poking out of the ground, jumbled rolls of fencing cast into woods, old fencing drooping on rotten posts, rickety gates hanging off hinges – it was as if the tenant farmers didn't care. And some didn't. They didn't own the land, so why should they? But some of the loose wire was lethal. I had seen a roe deer hopping helplessly through the heather with its hind leg caught in wire and we had found a dead sheep hanging by its neck from a fence, strangled in its panicked attempt to escape. And not all fences were what they appeared to be from the distance. Some had been clumsily doubled up and topped with barbed wire. Difficult to clear, as Biglie discovered to his detriment, when in mid-air the barb hooked viciously into the thin skin lining his balls. He let out a surprised yelp and then hung from the fence, upside down with his weight on his front paws, waiting patiently for help. While I carefully unhooked the grotesquely stretched skin of his tender parts he remained perfectly still and didn't even wince.

Then with a nudge of gratitude he scampered off and rolled in the long grass, relieved to be intact.

A spell of heavy wet weather filled the stream above our cottage and gouged out deep grooves in the track, sending a rush of water straight into the foundations. The land around was beginning to look like a cross-country circuit as our car slithered and slipped in the mud. We had to do something about it. Even though the land around us belonged to the Crown Estate, the Crown factors, with an air of disinterest, refused to assist with any maintenance of the track. So Jock, known locally as the 'digger-boy' as he operates a JCB, came to help us stem the flow. With deep concentration on his face, he sat at the controls of his huge orange machine putting it through its paces. Like a Jurassic monster, it planted its long clumsy-looking arm into the soil and, with the skill of a circus acrobat, could almost twirl right around, balancing its bulk in mid-air. It took two long days to dredge, dig and lay down piping and hardcore while we collected large stones to form the ramparts of a crude bridge over the stream.

Jock came into the kitchen for a cup of coffee. Inspired by the lukewarm attitude of the Crown factors, he and Jonathan were engaged in a favourite topic of many highlanders, the division of the Scots and the English, when our Amazonian house guest, an old friend of mine, burst into the room with just a short towel wrapped around her ample bosom. 'Oh, I'm such a slob,' she announced to the room in loud, London tones. Upstairs, I had suggested she might like to put on some clothes as we had company. 'Oh, I don't mind,' she had said breezily. But *he* might, I had tried to point out. 'Well he shouldn't,' she had retorted, without thinking. 'People should be used to bodies by now. It's the nineties for God's sake.' So she made her entrance with little more than nipple to navel covered, shuffling her bare thighs around the kitchen table to the bathroom door. If Jock had been eating, he would have choked. Instead, his pale beige pallor shifted to crimson. Born and raised in the Braes, he didn't know where to look. 'A friend of the wife?' he asked Jonathan finally. As if that explained it all. There were more important things to dwell on, though. At one of the nearby farms a calf had been born with two heads. 'You should stick that in your fucking camera, Jon,' Jock suggested, helpfully.

I woke up during the night and took a sip of water from the glass on the floor by my side of the bed. It tasted of soil. Must be peat in our water supply, I thought. After all that rain. And went back to sleep. In the early morning light, I rolled over and just happened to look at the glass. There was a large, dead worm floating in the little bit of brown water at the bottom. *Yuck*. I could taste the soil in my mouth again. I was sure the worm wasn't there when I had filled the glass from the tap. Perhaps it had slipped in during the night. But then again, perhaps not. Only the other day, Hamish had turned on his tap at Ladderfoot and a frog had plopped into his dram. 'Well, that's life in the country,' I announced coolly to Jonathan. 'What is?'

the motionless lump in the bed asked sleepily. 'A worm in my glass. A big, fat worm.' In a shot, he was on his feet, frantically checking every wrinkle in the sheets. I couldn't have got him out of bed faster if I'd set light to it. He loathes insects and worms. Things that fly and slither. One of his worst moments, a manic moment in India, was when he discovered that the large, dive-bombing moths he was getting accustomed to were, in fact, giant flying cockroaches.

'Yoohoo,' Pam called from the back door of Ladderfoot. The shrill call resounded in the air and stopped Jonathan in his tracks. He and Biglie were just on their way to the small, open dams at the foot of the hills. After the wet weather they would be overflowing with the fresh, peaty water that was gushing down the hill streams. Although the dams stored water to wash out the stills in the local distillery, they also served as Biglie's private pools. With his daily baths, his black coat gleamed with health and he smelled so clean and delectable. Like a crisp digestive biscuit.

'Hello, how lovely to see you,' Pam greeted Jonathan at the back door with a kettle in her hand. From head to calf her country lady's outfit was impeccable but, somewhat absurdly, her feet were tucked into two plastic supermarket bags, firmly tied at the ankles. 'I forgot to bring my walking shoes,' she explained with sunny grace, as if plastic bags were the next best thing. And on her, they were. She had been for a walk in the bags, she said, but wondered if Jonathan could just fill her kettle from the stream as she, in her smooth, plastic footwear, might slip in. He stayed for a cup of tea and attempted to persuade her that the next time she forgot something she should come and borrow from us. That's what neighbours are for.

Ben, a golden retriever, came to stay. He belonged to Ross Leckie, the author of *Hannibal*, *Scipio*, and *Carthage*, and had been Biglie's friend in Edinburgh. They had often romped together on Arthur's Seat and scattered the ducks in the pond. After an unexpected spat on the first day, they resumed their companionship and transformed our peace into a boisterous summer camp. Long walks with lots of hares and rabbits to chase. And long swims in the dams. Barely moving his legs, Ben glided, lazily, through the cold water while Biglie paddled himself across the dams like a competitive swimmer, his tail swishing above the surface in delight.

A walk over to the source of the Livet nearly put an end to their fun though when we ran into a pack of working dogs rounding up hill sheep. One of the dogs broke off from the pack and went straight for Ben's throat. Soft and good-natured, Ben was taken by surprise and yelped. Biglie, who had by now matured into a strong, fearless dog, dived in to protect Ben and would have done damage to the attacker if it had chosen to ignore the guttural yells emanating from a big, hairy, rather fierce-looking, figure in a string vest. The consequences must have been far worse than a bloody fight with Biglie as the dog, without a moment's hesitation, backed down and slunk away with its tail between its hind legs. The big man and his chunky brother or cousin, who was equally hairy, muttered gruffly to each other and, stabbing their crooks into the ground, strode off after the sheep, stopping momentarily for the chunky one to scoop up a lame ewe and fling it around his bare, square shoulders. At a glance, these men looked rough, close to the earth, lending credence to the myth of sheep-shagging, cow-tossing highlanders.

Further up the river, we came across another relative. Their father, perhaps. Drunk at the wheel of his battered Land Rover, he seemed to be driving aimlessly over the land that, presumably, he tenanted. He stopped right beside us, in the middle of a shallow section of the river, where we were hopping across stones to get to the other side. His wizened, blue-and-red face gazed at us through yellowed, watery eyes. Long strands of unkempt, white hair fell down past his shoulders like twists of rope framing his puffy, bruised-looking features. His breath reeked of cheap whisky. An old farmer, passing the time.

'It must have been a nice place to live,' Jonathan said, conversationally, pointing up to the abandoned cottage perched on the hillside above the Livet.

Situated over the boundary on the Glenfiddich Estate, it was indeed a beautiful spot with a clear south-westerly view to the Cairngorms. It had once been a keeper's cottage but, like so many of the remote highland properties that become victim to the greed of some landowners, it had lain dormant for years. Left to ruin and pilfer. Open to chancers willing to strip it of its recyclable parts. We thought of Alan and Dalla and the distance they had covered.

'Aye, it was a bonnie hoose alright,' the old farmer spouted, taking a swig from the quart bottle in his big, grubby hands. 'Until some bugger pinched the doors.'

The ponies raced on to the land around us. Up and down the hill. The foals bucked and kicked and frolicked in their new-found space. And the handsome, richly terracotta-toned stallion stood proud like a Red Indian with his long mane of black hair waving gently in the breeze. Curious by nature and in search of company, they seemed happiest hanging around our cottage. While the foals pulled the washing off the line and chewed the pegs, the stallion hung his big, beautiful head over the fence and snorted gently at Biglie. Feeling threatened, Biglie stood his ground and barked incessantly but, after watching the stallion relieve himself in one long, sonorous whoosh, he seemed to gain respect for the bigger beast and accepted his presence. On several occasions, I swear I saw them rub noses.

I was trying to retrieve my favourite pair of silky knickers from the grass-smeared jaws of a cheeky young colt when a convoy of four-wheel-drive vehicles rumbled along the track. A head at each window looked my way but only Sandy, the friendly keeper, waved. Of course, I whispered to the colt, it's the 'Glorious Twelfth'. Aren't you lucky you're not a grouse. Not even that thought made him relinquish my knickers so I resigned myself to finding them in the grass later, chewed and soggy, destined for the bin. I went inside to fetch the binoculars.

The vehicles left the track and drove up the hillside, depositing the rich clients at each butt. A sight that never fails to irritate me because I believe everything in the country should be worked for. Gone are the days of traditional sport when the keepers and clients themselves walked the hills and moors, raising the grouse with dogs. Now, the physical effort is more akin to a clay pigeon shoot and the fat and the unfit can blast the birds out of the sky before retiring for a big lunch.

I know because my brother and I used to work as grouse beaters on the Invercauld Estate. A group of us, mainly made up of young unemployed men, formed a line across the moor and set off at a cracking speed that had to be maintained through sinking, boggy moss and thigh-high heather, waving our white flags. These we learned were as much for beating the heather to raise the grouse as they were for signalling our positions to the more careless, trigger-happy clients, which was crudely brought home to us when a pellet whistled right through the peak of a friend's cap. Miraculously, his scalp was only grazed. Soaked with sweat and chilled in the persistent rain, we dragged our weary feet in their heavy boots to an exposed spot for a lunch of soggy spam sandwiches and cold, watery cocoa. The Estate obviously worked on the principle that we would be so ravenous from the physical exertion that we would eat anything. For, sitting some distance apart, in the shelter of a hut if the weather was bad, accompanied by their bejewelled, fur-clad women, the clients, who had been driven in comfort from butt to butt, were noisily tucking into game turines and plum brandy.

'Ishthagenatavgo?' Norman mumbled around the well-sucked pipe.

We drew a blank. Silence. Flummoxed by his strong accent we often took it in turns to stab at a reply but, on this occasion, we had absolutely no idea what he had just asked. We must have looked like a couple of turnips. He removed the pipe from his mouth for a moment and gestured with it towards Corrunich which was lit up like a Christmas tree.

'Is that a generator you've got?' he repeated slowly and deliberately, on the verge of losing patience. Fed up with having to repeat everything he said.

'Yes.' We nodded and smiled like mindless puppets, looking back at the cottage.

We had given in to modernisation and got it that morning. Six months after moving in. It was only a site generator, a noisy little machine, that gave off enough power for lights, a vacuum cleaner, a washing machine, and our newly-acquired computer, although none of them could be on at the same time. Most importantly, we had got it for the central heating we were planning to put in. But, as we had never seen the cottage lit up before, we had put all the lights on and wandered outside into the fading

71

dusk light to see what it looked like. All of a sudden, the absurdity of it hit me. There we were at the edge of the moor, admiring the cottage because it was lit up. And, while we were admiring it, we could see the lights beginning to dim. The fuel was running out. A highland farmer would never, needlessly, waste fuel like that.

'What kind is it?' Norman asked, ignoring the distant, irregular drone of the engine as it struggled to keep going.

'A Lombardini.'

'How much did you pay for that?'

Jonathan just looked at him and smiled. The locals always wanted to know how much we paid for everything. Either gauging how much money we had or how much we wasted.

'A lot less than the hydro want for mains electricity,' he conceded.

'How much do those buggers want?'

'Close to seventeen thousand pounds.'

Norman's eyebrows jumped in astonishment.

'And four thousand of that is for so-called future maintenance,' I pointed out.

'Ach, the crooks,' he uttered, spitting out a bit of tobacco.

Scandalous, daylight robbery, we all agreed, shaking our heads in disbelief. Who had that kind of money? For a facility most people took for granted. We certainly didn't. Neither did the locals. They had all relied on generators, right up to the late 1970s, when a hydro scheme brought electricity to the Braes for a few hundred pounds per house. Corrunich, which wasn't lived in at that time, missed out.

'Maintenance.' He spat the word out, pronouncing each syllable with emphasis. 'What maintenance? They won't even fix the lines in winter. Too much snow on the ground.'

It wasn't long before we were without power again. Shame faced, Jonathan had to go to Charlie Skene, the Tomintoul mechanic, and admit that he had managed to get a cloth sucked into the engine of the generator. He had been cleaning it while the engine was still running and it had gobbled up the cloth. A grin cracked across Charlie's oil-spattered, good-looking features and then he laughed out loud. Right from the bottom of his belly. His lively, azure eyes indicated that he had seen it all before. 'Here, take my spanner kit,' he said in his strong, fast-spoken accent, the words often difficult to catch. 'And I'll see you in a week.' Charlie was used to coping. Born and raised in a big family just outside Tomintoul where his father had been the forester, Charlie could turn his big hands to many things. And he encouraged his own three young boys to do the same. Competent with power tools and welding equipment, they had skilfully fashioned carts and bikes out of scrap metal and dumped engines. And the eldest had 'the touch'. Some farmers insisted that only he should fix their engines. The fact that he was ten years old seemed irrelevant. 'It's the only way to learn,' reasoned Charlie, who always had a practical air about him. And

Jonathan welcomed the opportunity to learn. Even if it took him the whole week, he would be forced to take the generator apart and put it back together again.

We watched the first group walk hesitatingly across the moor. They had paid a fee to walk up the track to see the highland ponies. A family: two adults and three children. Alone. The adults hung back and let the children roam amongst all those long, stamping legs and nipping teeth. Unsure, the stallion pricked back his ears and snorted at the little people. It was like watching fools enter a lion's cage. Little squeals and awkward movements. The stallion looked as if he was ready to charge or kick. He had mares and foals to protect.

We found ourselves glued to the window of the room that was to be our sitting-room. We had just ripped the soaked, mouldy plaster off the dripping gable-end wall and had discovered the original hearth. But, the scene on the moor had us transfixed. Helplessly. *Move away from the legs*. We didn't have a telephone. *Stop waving your arms*. If anything happened, we would have to jump into the car and head for help. *Get out of there*. Oh, where was the ranger's wife?

Thank God, they've come to their senses. The adults seemed to be calling to the children. Slowly, two of them pulled away. The remaining one stood rigid in the tangle of legs. He screamed then dashed towards his parents. So did the foals. This was a good game. The stallion trotted around the perimeter of his group, whinnying, as the foals chased the family out of the gate. No blood, no wounds, just one frightened, lucky family. We withdrew from the window and resumed work on the wall, checking the granite stonework. It needed a little re-pointing but once it was cleaned we would leave it bare and build a fireplace in the stone hearth.

The second group arrived by Land Rover. As usual, the ponies were gathered around our washing-line, chewing pegs and tugging at the clothes. The ranger's wife could have called the ponies over to the Estate gate, as she often did, but she chose to drive the group right up to our fence. The group, a mixed bunch, showed surprisingly little interest in the ponies and focused their attention on our humble home. Feeling that sting of unwelcome intrusion, I slunk back into the shadows of the back door. Like a caged animal. I couldn't understand these people. They had paid to see some sprite, friendly highland ponies in their natural habitat with a guide who was so calm with them that they could stroke the animals in safety, but they were more interested in snapping me and my home. People like that, with their cameras shamelessly aimed into my privacy and their loud voices shattering the peace, are always brave behind a lens when faced with the unknown. It doesn't matter if it's 'tribal woman suckling her baby in Africa' or 'highland woman shrinking into the doorway of her croft', as long as the photo is in the album, there is proof of adventure.

'Rolling, rolling, rolling. Raw hide.' Jonathan was outside,

singing at the top of his voice. He was standing in front of the barn door on a raised cobbled area that he had come to regard as his stage. The sheep were his audience. Singing and talking to himself are part of his nature so, when he's tinkering with something in the barn, he often pops on to his imaginary stage for a burst of song.

On this occasion, I was upstairs in our office writing letters as part of our market research but I couldn't resist peeking at him. I climbed on to the desk and shoved my head out of the skylight window. '*Rolling, rolling, rolling* . . .' He was in full swing, building up to his dramatic crescendo. I looked at the sheep in the field below us. They were chomping mindlessly to the notes of the energetic tenor. I looked over to the sheep in the field on the far side of the barn. They were moving to the rhythm. Towards Jonathan. Surely not, I thought. And then I felt my cheeks burn. Oh my God, there was a group of people strolling behind them. That's why the sheep were moving. We had heard that John Stuart had relatives visiting from Australia. And here they were, practically in our garden, as the farmer showed them his tenanted land.

I had to stop Jonathan. I had lived with him long enough to know exactly what he was going to do next. So that the farmer and his relatives wouldn't understand what I was saying, I shouted to him in Turkish. He looked up at me, smiled, and carried on singing. He thought I was kidding. Again, I tried to warn him. He was on his last '*raw hide*', holding the last note, popping open the buttons on his jeans. The farmer and his relatives had come to a halt, looking our way. Please, just look to your right, I pleaded. He did. And, desperately embarrassed, leapt back into the darkness of the barn. Standing stock-still for a moment before leading his relatives up the field, John Stuart, who we had barely talked to, must have been wondering what kind of madness had come to inhabit Corrunich. As for the sheep, they escaped a mooning that day.

'Well, well,' greeted the familiar choppy tones of our pipe-smoking friend at the gate.

'It's a lovely evening,' Jonathan said.

We had been admiring the deep mango glow settling on the hills. Soon it would climb over the tops and blend into translucent streaks of papaya pink. And finally, in a last defiant burst, it would explode into brilliant vermilion before fading through shades of purple from the sky. Evenings like this filled us with a warm joy and made us feel we lived in one of the most beautiful places on earth.

'Aye, just you wait 'til winter.' His eyes twinkled playfully with the knowledge of what lay in store.

It was time to heat up the old lady. All the signs were there. Shunting aside the warmth of the short highland summer, a definite chill had hit the air. Cold winds and rain. Sometimes sleet. The rowans were full and the leaves and grasses were turning. Farmers had begun to gather sheep off the hills. The geese had passed overhead on their route south. And there was talk of forthcoming storms and a long harsh winter. In fact, it felt like it could snow any minute. Weather for birch fires, fruitcake and a dram. Preferably, a cask strength Ardbeg warmed in the hand.

Heating up the old lady meant putting in central heating for the first time. We already had the generator for the pump but we didn't think the ancient solid-fuel Raeburn could cope. Besides, it was proving laborious. It required constant stoking. Which was fine if we were at home all day but, if we went away for any length of time, we returned to a cold cottage. So we and the solid-fuel stove parted company and an oil-fed, but equally ancient, one was put in its place. This meant we had to buy another big, ugly tank – we already had one storing diesel for the generator – in which to store the kerosene. With both tanks standing dutifully by the gate, like glum sentries, we were all set for the heating system. A gravity-fed one, as it had to continue working when the generator was off. But who could put in such a system? At a reasonable price. John Hammond, the agent who had sold us Corrunich and his Welsh wife, Karon, would know. They had since become friends and partners in greed around the kitchen table, tucking into tasty dishes and bottles of wine as we all listened to John's passionate stories about past adventures in the Hindu Kush and Afghanistan. He was an Englishman by birth but a highlander at heart. A skilled hunter who took excited Spaniards stalking in the hills. And in the spirit of the few people who have really travelled with the wind, relying on one's own resources and taking people as they come, he could fit in anywhere and talk to anyone. In his role as estate agent, Estate manager, shooting tenant, and all-round affable chap, he knew the farmers, keepers and tradesmen in the area. So he knew just the man for us.

Pint-sized and middle-aged, with buoyant, coiffed blond hair, Peter Hunter stepped out of his van in a pair of small Cuban-heeled boots. A Freddie Starr look-alike. Over the roof of his low-set van, which met his chin, he smiled hello and then promptly sank from view. Slightly concerned, we peeped around the bonnet to see if he was all right. He was. On his hands and knees getting acquainted with Biglie. He loved animals, he said. He couldn't even bear to kill a mouse. When his mother had asked him to deal with the mice in her house, he had left cheese out for them so that they wouldn't get hungry. Recognising a respect for animals that was tantamount to soppy, Biglie followed his new friend around for the next few days, nudging his bum with his nose and humping him whenever he bent over. 'Ach, you stupid pup,' Peter would say, playfully slapping him away.

The route of the gravity-fed system seemed to frustrate Peter. Relentlessly. He would scratch his puzzled brow and sigh wearily, as if working out a complicated sum in his head. At lunchtime, he would retire to his van to think it through with the aid of a cigarette which never failed to put him to sleep. One afternoon, when I noticed his motionless body slumped over the steering-wheel, I hesitated to wake him up. But I was convinced he was dead so I gave him a little shake. Just exhausted, he admitted, bashfully, stretching and yawning at the same time. He was a moonlighter – couldn't say no to a job.

He returned a week later, dressed in a suit and Cuban heels, to deliver his bill. Over a dram, he remarked on the cowboy boots that he had seen in our bedroom. They had reminded him of his cowboy gear at home. Upstairs in the privacy of his bedroom, he would don Stetson hat and Cuban heels and, with his gun hanging from the belt around his waist, he would stand with his feet apart and practice twirling and firing his gun in front of the mirror. Downstairs, his wife and daughters, watching television in the sitting-room, would look at one another in familiar amusement as the gun repeatedly clattered to the floor above their heads. Dad's dropped it again, they would say. 'But I'm in great demand as the Milkybar Kid at the fancy dress parties and pantomimes,' chuckled the ageless Peter of Dufftown.

Hamish, our part-time neighbour, turned up at the back door holding a brace of pheasant. He had just shot them and tied their feet together, ready to hang for a few days. Thrilled at the prospect of eating wild pheasant, Jonathan and I immediately discussed how we would cook them. Roasted on a bed of root vegetables or, perhaps, gently cooked in red wine. Hamish suggested we just eat the breasts. But, first, we had to pluck them. On this, Hamish could offer no advice as his butcher, who always prepared the pheasant for him, used a plucking machine.

Two days later, we spread some newspaper over the kitchen table and set about plucking and gutting the rather beautiful pheasant. It was a messy process. The soft, fluffy under-feathers took to the air and landed in the pans, the fruit bowl, and on to a fascinated Biglie who was watching from his bed. Over the last two days, he had stopped regularly to sniff the dangling feet of these birds as they hung by their necks from hooks in the back porch. His nose twitched expectantly. The contents of their stomachs revealed a last meal of wild berries and, once thoroughly denuded, the birds looked rather skimpy. A bird each and some for Biglie. Roasted, stuffed with breadcrumbs and herbs, they were deliciously gamy.

Hamish arrived at the back door again, holding a single pheasant. He had knocked it over on the road. We decided to cut off the breasts this time and create an Indian-style aromatic dish with them. But, out of the blue, Alex and Anne Caroline turned up to stay. Childhood sweethearts and old friends from my days at university, they live in Edinburgh. He's English and she's half French but they love Scotland and have travelled almost every inch of it, camping in the mist and the rain. And they fitted into our highland lifestyle with panache, always bearing edible goodies from the city. This time it was eight pheasant breasts.

So now we had ten breasts and four hungry people. Alex fancied a pheasant pie. A big, classic one with puff pastry. I agreed to make a pie but, thankfully, as it is not one of my favourite tasks, there was not enough time to make a puff pastry so I opted for a choux instead. Not convinced that it would be as nice, a disgruntled Alex poured himself a glass of wine and slumped beside a bowl of olives while I cut the breasts into thin strips and sautéed them in olive oil with garlic, onions and peppers. I smiled to myself as I poured in a generous quantity of red wine. Alex wouldn't be disappointed for long. He was one of the few people I really enjoyed cooking for. He just loved food. In a noisily appreciative, plate-licking way. In went the plum tomatoes, whatever herbs we had growing in pots, and a good grind of seasoning before spooning the mixture into the middle of a ring of choux which would expand and puff up in the oven. A kind of *gougère* of pheasant. Alex was speechless when it came to the table.

The next morning, we began the day with a hearty Canadian breakfast of thin pancakes with bacon and maple syrup to send us off on a long walk into the hills. As we were putting our boots on, I noticed Alex was busy over by the sink. His back was to us. Do you need a hand? I asked, wondering what he was doing. He swivelled around and grinned sheepishly, red sauce smeared around his lips. *Alex!* A mock scolding in a French accent – Anne Caroline tends to lapse into French when scolding or losing patience with her unpredictable husband. Who, at that moment, was greedily tucking into the leftover pheasant pie. Embarrassed at having been caught, he hastily covered up the remains and wiped his hands on his trousers. Let's go for a walk, he said, heading out the door. But we had only walked a few miles when Alex started badgering us. 'The weather's coming in,' he announced, looking at the sky with a degree of hope. 'Don't you think we should head back and finish that pie?'

*

An elderly man, with a pack on his back, came off the hill with a youthful fitness to his stride. Using his walking stick like a paddle he had obviously worked himself into a rhythm and stuck to it. His back arched slightly from the weight on his back and he held his head forwards like the prow of a ship. A determined posture. I guessed he had walked over the hills from Strathdon and was now heading to a meeting point. A man with a sense of purpose.

He hadn't seen the ponies. But the stallion had seen him. He shook his long, black mane in a challenging fashion and commenced a lethargic charge. At the sound of the hooves beating up the ground, the old man's stride broke into a run. His stick flailing in the air, he ran awkwardly, hampered by the burden on his back and the uneven ground. I felt my hand slap over my mouth as I held my breath. *He could twist an ankle or, worse, have a heart attack.* Again, I found myself watching helplessly. Not only did we not have a phone but, on this occasion, we couldn't even rush out for help. Our car, which had taken a severe beating from the rutted track, was sitting at Charlie's in Tomintoul.

The old man was almost at the gate but the stallion was rapidly closing the gap. Although running away was the worst thing he could do, I silently urged the old man on. *Run, run, run.* He reached the gate and climbed over it, dropping to the other side in exhaustion. I cheered out loud. He had made it, unharmed. The stallion stood menacingly by the gate for a moment and then dropped his head to graze. To him, it had all been a bit of mischievous fun.

A few weeks later we found ourselves at the Enterprise Board staring at the counsellor in silence. Our mouths must have hung open in horror. We had come to present our plan for the barn conversion and photography workshops. And he had completely missed the point.

'The way I see it,' he had just said. 'Is to open up the barn to bus parties and offer tea and cakes.'

Why does it always come to this? Tea and cakes? Tartan and cheap knick-knacks? Can't people see beyond bus parties in the highlands?

'Of course,' he went on, pleased with his suggestion. 'You would have to tarmac your track and put in disabled toilets.'

A rash of irritation was beginning to itch my skin. We were talking about photography workshops. Exclusive, black and white photography workshops. Not a tourist attraction. The whole point was that the workshops would be in a place of great beauty. Quiet light and shifting landscapes, a spiritual haven for creativity. We had a file full of letters from fellow photographers and from established workshops in America keen to join forces. But the concept seemed to zoom over the head of this counsellor. For the Enterprise scheme there would have to be more to it than that. We had to go back to the drawing-board and come up with a more decisive business plan.

*

I walked back from the phone box, feeling rather sad and pensive. Our first freelance project had come to an abrupt end. It was to have been a glossy photographic book on Scotland. Jonathan was to take the photographs, our friend Ross Leckie was to write the text and I was to co-ordinate (whatever that means). And the entire project was to be sponsored by one of the oldest whisky companies in Scotland. But the chairman had just died. A routine operation with a tragic ending. Not long ago, we had sat in a meeting with him and he had seemed full of life. A well known and highly respected publisher had agreed to fly up from London to meet him and discuss the cost and format of the book but, with the loss of the chairman, the company wasn't keen to carry on. So the project died too. One thing was starkly clear though, life can be capricious so we had to make the most of it every day. After all, it may be the only life we get.

'We're off to India,' we told Norman at the gate.

'India?' His eyebrows arched in amazement. It wasn't every day that someone from the Braes went to India. In fact, Norman rarely left the Braes.

'India,' he repeated slowly, chewing the syllables as if enjoying the sound. 'Why?'

'We've got the chance to take some photographs over there,' Jonathan replied, simply.

'And does somebody pay for that?' Ever the canny highlander.

'Just the flights.' It was not a glamorous assignment.

'So, how do you get about?' he asked, stuffing the tobacco into his pipe.

Things are so cheap, we explained. Trains, buses, rooms. Norman looked lost. He had seen images on television but to physically imagine being there was beyond his realms. Tomintoul, at times, seemed a world away to him.

'We were wondering if you could keep an eye on Corrunich for us,' Jonathan asked. 'There shouldn't be anyone there while we're away.'

'Aye, I'll be glad to,' Norman said, with a mischievous smile. 'If I see anyone, I'll just wander over there with my shotgun.'

As he guffawed through his pipe smoke, we parted with visions of unsuspecting visitors blasted into oblivion. Body parts and scraps of clothing dangling from the few trees in our garden. A hapless encounter with Norman and his shotgun.

'I swear I smell whisky in the air,' Jonathan said with characteristic pleasure, as we stepped off the plane at Inverness airport six weeks later.

After the dust and heat of India, it was refreshing to feel the chill air tingle on our suntanned skin. Our senses were acute, recharged by sandalwood, coconut oil, fresh curry leaves, mimosa and sweet-scented jasmine. Heading home we passed a vehicle crawling along the edge of the busy road. An industrial cleaner, sweeping and sucking up litter. Having just shared the streets with crowds of people, buses, cars, bicycles, camels, cows, horses, dogs, cats, monkeys, and the occasional elephant, this sight was extraordinary. Only in the West. A world away the people and animals lived amongst the litter. Some even lived off it.

I will never forget the skinny Indian who crept out of the shadows beside the wretched-looking skeleton of a dog. I had felt sorry for the dog and had thrown it some biscuits. As I stood back, the man, who was just as wretched-looking, picked up a crumpled paper bag and knelt down in front of the dog. He lay the paper bag on the ground, between him and the dog, and smoothed it out like a table-cloth. Then he gathered up the broken biscuits and placed them on the bag. Together, he on one side, the dog on the other, they shared the biscuits. I tried not to stare but I remember feeling so utterly humbled in the face of such hunger and dignity.

We picked up Biglie and embarked on the final leg home. The closer we got, the heavier the snow. Winter had hit the Braes and dumped all the snow on our track. As we drove around to Norman's farm to collect our post, we could see that the track was impassable. The snow had drifted in sections, covering the fences. We would have to put on our rucksacks, filled with Indian spices, and trek home.

Flanked by a jabbering posse of geese and ducks, a couple of curious turkeys met us in Norman's slushy yard. No one seemed to be around the barns, so we knocked on the back door. A gang of barking dogs gathered on the other side, ready to shoot out. The door was opened by a tough-looking woman with a pleasant, weather-beaten face. Norman's *bidie'in*. Although he had told us he lived alone, we had heard that he, in fact, lived with a woman.

'Here's your post,' she said, thrusting a plastic bag into my hands. 'It was damp but I dried it out on the radiator.'

Several cats slipped out of the doorway as she shouted at the six or seven dogs sniffing around our legs. Behind us, our car rocked on its wheels. Biglie was defending his confined space.

'*He*'s about somewhere,' Norman's *bidie'in* added, looking over to the sheep and cows tucking into hay around the barns.

And, as if he had heard her, *he* appeared. Dressed in his usual attire of a ripped shirt, baggy dungarees, a hat and big rubber boots, Norman waved his pipe in the air and squished his way through the slush and mud towards us with his crook hooked over one arm. Hoping for more food, the cows and sheep followed him. They were close to skin and bone but, compared to the emaciated, disease-ridden animals in the streets of India, they looked positively blooming.

'And how was your trip?' Norman asked, brightly. He seemed genuinely pleased to see us.

Interesting, inspiring, uplifting, exhausting. And cows are revered in India, we told him. In fact, we had a meal next to a man who had ordered two plates of food, one for himself and the other for the cow scavenging through the litter nearby. Norman was tickled pink.

We could hear the unmistakable chug of an old tractor. Biglie, who had heard it too, jumped out of his bed and barked at the back door. Outside the icy blizzard was getting thicker by the minute. We couldn't see beyond our gate but we could hear the coughing and spluttering as it got closer. As I let Biglie out, the blizzard blew in through the doorway and with it came Norman, clutching a wet plastic bag. The broken cab on his tractor was only partially weatherproof, so his beard and eyebrows were frozen white. He looked like a walrus.

'More post,' he said, handing over the bag as he shook the snow off himself and on to the kitchen floor. His rubber boots and dungarees were covered in sheep shit.

'*She* forgot to give it to you the other day,' he explained. 'It was drying on a radiator.'

'And what's *her* name?' I asked, removing the post from the bag. After the trip through the blizzard, it was sodden once more.

'What do you want to know her name for?' he teased, gruffly. 'She's just a silly bugger with a face.'

I laughed. We all did. It was his way. He sat down and took a dram. A double, at least. The kitchen filled with his strong pipe smoke. And, at one point, he tilted his head and spat on the stone floor. A big globule of tobacco-stained mucus. With dumb reticence, we pretended not to notice. We were just happy to have him in our home. Most of the local farmers were too shy or suspicious to come near. Nine drams later he was ready to go.

The blizzard had grown fierce, blowing hard snow in all directions like clouds of stinging pellets. We put on our hats, gloves and Gore-Tex jackets and walked outside with Norman who must have been fired from the spirit within for he seemed remarkably oblivious to the storm. In just a shirt and dungarees. And, of course, his hat. He doesn't go anywhere without his hat. With a big grin on his face, he clambered into the tractor cab, steered off the track and got stuck in the deep stream that was buried under the snow.

'It's difficult to see where you're going in this weather,' Jonathan said when he approached Norman to see if he could give him a hand.

'Aye, that's what it is,' he agreed, tipsily, and set off at a cracking pace to get another tractor from the farm and find his brother to help him.

He looked like a bear with a mission. A baggy figure, hunched from the cold, merging with the blizzard into a fuzzy blur. We had never seen him move so fast, almost running, using his crook as a stick. Ever since a bale of hay had fallen off a truck and squashed him, knocking his hip out of its socket, he had walked with a limp. But, we had heard, when he's on the scent of a deer, there's no one as fast as him. More remarkably, he never complains of the pain.

When we got back from shopping it was dark. But the night sky was clear. It had taken us all day to walk down to the car, drive the forty miles to town, shop, and drive back. And we still had to stuff the bags of shopping into rucksacks and walk through the snow. Over the hill to our isolated home. 'We really should harness Biglie,' Jonathan said, as we staggered like pack-mules through the sinking snow while Biglie bounded around chasing the rabbits that darted into the woods.

Jonathan's pack was full of tins of dog food and cartons of UHT milk. Mine was lighter with vegetables and fruit. He had shoved a bottle of wine into each pocket of his jacket and somewhere around the region of my ample bosom I had miraculously found room for a bottle of whisky. On either side, we were weighed down by a clutch of plastic bags that hadn't fitted into the packs. We were accustomed to the weight on our backs but, with each step, the bulging supermarket bags banged awkwardly against our shins, the handles cutting into our fingers. And there was still more in the car. Supplies for a month. Which Jonathan would fetch the next day.

'Yeah, he should earn his keep,' I muttered breathlessly, stumbling and sinking into the puffy drifts. They were crusty on top and soft underneath. Like a good meringue.

It was too late, we both knew that. He should have been harnessed as a puppy if that's what we had intended. A skidoo might be useful, we mused. In the right conditions. An eight-wheeled Hill Cat might be better. The keepers use them uphill over heather and snow. A pony would be more traditional. And in keeping with the environment. Or a reindeer.

We reached the end of the plantation and entered our isolated glen lit up by a full, diaphanous moon which was suspended over Corrunich like a beacon to guide us home. No other lights could be seen. Just the bright moon in a starry sky above the crusty sea of snow that flowed without a break into frozen, white hills. Our faces glowed in the silvery-blue moonlight, the icy air freshening our skin. A perfect winter night. Still and quiet. We had never felt so alive.

But, in the highlands, it never stays perfect for long. In the early hours of the following morning, the wind whipped up into a frenzy. It howled around the trees outside our bedroom window and blew through the slates on the roof and down the pipes. It sounded like a high-speed train blaring its horn through a tunnel. With no insulation in the roof and ill-fitting windows, our bedroom was so well-ventilated that, during the night, we had put on thermals and jumpers. The morning light revealed a white-out. We couldn't even see the barn from the cottage. And the wind was still beating and pounding the air, like an angry beast.

Reluctantly, Jonathan put on his hat and ski goggles and stepped into the storm with Biglie. Within seconds they were swallowed up by the whiteness. They knew their way across the moor to the track and then the long walk down to the car but, even so, I worried. It was so easy to get disoriented in this weather, even on home territory. However, if they managed to get the rest of the shopping, we could hole up for a month if we had to.

Mission completed, they returned about two hours later. Exhausted. And white. As if they had been blasted in snow. Only their brown eyes were visible. Biglie's looked pleadingly towards his bed. Jonathan's creased into a smile that said *I must be crazy*. With his moustache and beard encased in icicles, I couldn't resist telling him that he reminded me of a soulful-looking Arctic baboon that I had seen in the *National Geographic*.

A few days later the storm settled down and the sunrise struck the hilltops with pools of liquid orange tinged with pink, like painted finger-nails on frozen hands. The evidence of the storm's havoc was imprinted on the lopsided landscape. The snow had been pushed into solid, uneven mounds, like lifeless waves. Our gate was buried under a three-foot ramp of snow and the drifts around the barn were so high that we could walk on to the roof and then slide down again. Biglie enjoyed it too, pausing for a moment on the rooftop to survey the scene. In the fields below him, the cocky hares in their white winter coats teased him as they calmly scrabbled for food. He barked into the air sending them racing in all directions. They were gone by the time he had slid down the snow-chute.

We ventured on to the hill for a bit of ungainly, gung-ho skiing. It was hardly a good mogul run, more like a slalom obstacle course, but we did find a few patches we could use as virgin piste. The bright sunshine radiated an invigorating warmth. The snow sparkled like phosphorescence in the sunlight. And gentle gusts raised dustings of powder snow into the air, skimming them along the surface like dancing phantoms. It was all so magical. The calm after the storm. Like the sudden burst of bloom after the rains on the parched African plains. Moments that you never forget. Cut off in our snow-bound glen, it was like having our own little adventure. Not the intrepid, soul-searching kind of Benedict Allen or Robyn Davidson. But an adventure all the same.

Jonathan's parents came for Christmas. All the way from Istanbul. Their first experience of winter in Scotland and only their second visit to the highlands (the first was our wedding in Braemar). And the weather performed in style. Another dump of snow and a raging blizzard causing hazardous driving conditions. Jonathan picked them up at Inverness airport and could barely make out the road home.

At the bottom of the track, they bundled up in warm clothing and boots and stepped out into the wild night. Jonathan filled his backpack with their hand luggage and the extra clothing he had brought for them. Then he tied rope around their big, heavy suitcases and, like two huskies, he and his father pulled them blindly through the snow. His mother followed slowly behind with the only light they had. A dim torch.

Waiting anxiously with Biglie in the warmth of the kitchen, I was making a hot, nourishing meal, listening to road reports on the radio. About three hours later than expected, I saw a faint beam of torchlight on the horizon.

Way over by the plantation. As the blizzard was beginning to recede, I was confident they would be able to make out the lights of the cottage from there so I put on my boots and Gore-Tex and headed out to help. I had only gone about a hundred metres when I fell, giggling, into the stream still flowing beneath the snow. I had thought I was on the track. Biglie's bark echoed through the snowy darkness so I aimed for the sound and bumped into Jonathan's father steaming towards the lights of Corrunich, pulling a suitcase. Jonathan had apparently gone back to help his mother who was struggling through the snow as the torch batteries had run out. When they eventually got to the back door, his mother was exhausted and freezing. About to collapse. So we peeled off her sodden fur coat, ushered her into a steaming hot bath and, after a cup of tea, she went to bed. To this day, I am still amazed that she even made it as, for some reason only known to her, she had refused the wellies on offer and had tottered all the way through the snow in a pair of high-heeled shoes that she had zipped into ankle-high, see-through, plastic galoshes.

Jonathan's mother was still with us, his father had returned to Istanbul, when the colours of the rainbow illuminated the south-western night sky. Stars flashing pink, yellow, green and blue. Like a great black dome inlaid with sparkling jewels that were so low we could pluck them out of their mould. If we hadn't been driven out by cigarette smoke to get some air, we might have missed them. But Jonathan's mother is a heavy smoker and, although we could tolerate it in places like Istanbul where everyone moves in a cloud of cigarette smoke, in the fresh highland air it seemed to invade every orifice, making us hot and prickly and prone to headaches. So, no matter what the weather, to step outside was a relief. To step outside and witness such a sky was hypnotic. We turned off the generator to watch it in complete silence and Jonathan dashed indoors to get his mother. Finding it too cold, she poked her head out of the window for a few seconds. Yes, lovely darling, she said, and darted back inside. She was right, it was cold. In fact, it was bloody freezing. But, like two pillars of ice, we stood our ground. This kind of magic was part of being here. You just wouldn't see such a sight in the city. And we have never seen it again.

In the new year, we woke up to find a coating of snow over our bed. The direction of the wind had changed and blown fine snow through the rickety skylight windows. And we could hear a constant drip of water. It was coming through the hatch to the loft. The pool of water forming on the landing below indicated that the loft must be full of melting snow. I went downstairs to let Biglie out and opened the inner back door to a wall of snow. It had filled the whole back porch area. Biglie pounced into it with all four paws and we tunnelled our way to the back door. The wall of snow on the outside was less impressive as the wind had beaten it down. I punched a hole in it and Biglie jumped through, clearing it like a circus hoop.

Jonathan emptied the loft of snow, filling buckets and

bin bags, while I shovelled the snow out of the back porch. We then mopped all the water up with towels and put our bedding over the radiator to dry. Finally, I put the coffee on and began to set the table for breakfast. You'll never guess what, Jonathan said, when he came into the kitchen. What? The hot water's finished, he said, grinning. As Alan and Dalla had installed a Valiant water heater that ran off large propane gas cylinders, that meant dragging the empty cylinder down the snowy track and then dragging a full one back up. Tiring, impractical and expensive but we couldn't afford to change the system.

We lay the tall gas cylinder on its side and tied some rope around the end. Together, we tugged. It budged sluggishly. The deep snow was hard in parts, soft in others. We rose and sank, rose and sank, and tugged and pulled until we reached the car. That was the easy part. A full cylinder was going to be hard work. With the back seats down, the cylinder lay diagonally across the Subaru. Biglie had to share the front seat with me. Jonathan put the key in the ignition. The car wouldn't move. The wheels had frozen to the snow. So we all piled out and dug the snow away from the wheels. Back inside, we rocked and revved *Thunk*. The wheels loosened. We were off.

'I don't believe it,' Jonathan said, banging the steering-wheel with his fist. What? 'We've run out of petrol,' he said, as we ground to a halt a mile outside Tomintoul. For weeks, the red light had been flashing continually on the petrol gauge, even when we filled the tank up. It was a minor problem really and so we had ignored it but, obviously, somewhere along the line we had miscalculated. It's just not our day, Jonathan concluded, shaking his head in disbelief. I smiled. There was no point getting worked up about it. We simply weren't prepared for winter. We didn't have the money to lay in supplies and fix all engines and appliances. We just had to take each day as it came. Like everyone else around us did.

The three of us began to walk the mile to Tomintoul where there was a petrol station. We hoped it was open, more often it was closed. We waved down the only car that came speeding along the empty road. It was Billy Strachan, the builder, who originally hailed from Glasgow with his Connolly-style humour intact. He screeched to a halt and we hopped aboard as he tossed Tammy, a rather matted Scottie dog into the back. Some years ago, shaggy little Tammy, named after Tammy Wynette, had been dumped with him as part-payment for a building job. He would have preferred cash but Tammy remained. Billy didn't have any spare petrol and nor did his son who happened to be driving the other way. Leaning out of the window, Billy had asked him if he had any. Half a tank, his son had said, looking at his own gauge. No, you pillock, Billy laughed. *Spare* petrol. Neither of them had any empty containers. Nor did we. So Billy dropped us off at the village petrol station which, fortunately, was open. No one there had an empty container either so we walked down the main street and knocked on a few doors. Delighted to help, an elderly woman parted with a plastic bottle that once contained washing detergent. We filled it with petrol, walked back to the car and poured it in. Just enough juice to get us in to Tomintoul to fill the tank up.

We then went on to Charlie Skene's. His mother sold the gas cylinders but she wasn't there so one of Charlie's boys gave us the keys and we swapped our empty for a full one. The Subaru sank under its weight and we added to it, ready for the journey home. An arduous journey. Dragging the obstinate cylinder uphill, through the snow in the dark. The whole day had gone. And when we got home, the generator wouldn't start. Jonathan cranked it and cursed. Cranked and cursed. Until the sweat was dripping off his forehead. He gave up and we lit a Tilly lamp instead. Unaware that we were about to embark on a long period without electricity.

Exhausted, we sat down to a bowl of pasta and a game of backgammon in candlelight. It had been one of those days when nothing goes according to plan. That was the only thing that was certain. We called it 'the Corrunich factor' and, later, when we shared some of our experiences with Alan and Dalla, they commented on how laid-back we seemed to be about it. 'Alan and I used to think it was some great conspiracy against us,' admitted Dalla. 'And we'd have to go to the Pole Inn and drown our sorrows.'

'People don't realise how hard it is to live up there,' acknowledged Charlie Skene, crouching over our generator.

For two days Jonathan had tried to fix it. For two days I had watched him swear and howl to the wind. Being rather incompetent with engines, I could offer no help. Finally, with mounting frustration, he had succumbed to the tormenting nature of the machine. It had to go to Charlie. What would we do without Charlie? But first we had to get it to him. A new fall of snow had buried the track beneath four-foot drifts and the car was at the bottom. We waited for a few days to see if the snow would thaw a little. It didn't. But with temperatures well below freezing, it did firm up in parts. So, like two medieval oxen, we pulled our heavy burden through the snow. Sometimes backwards, sometimes facing forwards, every inch of our bodies straining to the point of feeling sick. It took about four hours to get to the bottom of the track. And we were physically exhausted.

'You have to be driven and have big hearts,' Charlie went on, perhaps a touch nostalgically. 'You're lucky you both have the same dreams. It would be impossible to live so cut off if you had different minds.'

He knew what he was talking about. As a boy, he had lived a rustic existence, walking through miles of snow-drifts to school. He had shot deer and rabbits in the woods and, for a change of diet, his father would travel to the coast and swap a haunch of venison for fresh sea fish. As a young man, Charlie had spent the stalking season in the hills working the highland ponies which were used to carry the shot deer off the hill. Now Charlie's days were spent in the garage. A rural mechanic never gets a break. A rural mechanic who is also a fireman never gets a rest. But his heart was in the wilds. He wasn't alone. Living in a remote place appeals to a lot of men. Again, it's that passion for adventure. The challenge of coping in the wilderness, beating one's chest, chopping wood and building fires. The dream of capturing the shadow of Huckleberry Finn. Something like that.

'It's lovely,' agreed Jonathan. 'But it can be a pain in the arse at times.'

'Well, now you know why people chose to leave those crofts,' Charlie laughed, sympathetically. 'It wasn't just the Clearances. Some of them left at the first opportunity because it was so hard. Their hearts weren't in it.'

'I've been thinking about your bottom,' the doctor said, matter-of-factly, down the phone.

Jonathan tried to suppress his laughter. And snorted. If anyone had been listening in, they would have had fodder for colourful rumour.

As we didn't have a phone, the doctor had called one of the Braes' farmers who had sent his son on a skidoo across the fields and up the track to Corrunich. It was dark, well after six in the evening, so we had feared it must be urgent. Jonathan had been suffering from a discomfort that he had already taken to the doctor earlier that day. A thrombosed pile. Heaving the generator down the track had, quite literally, been a pain in the arse. Now we were back at the entrance to the Braes, huddled in the dull, yellow light of the breezy phone box, surrounded by empty, snow-blown fields. A stone's throw from the Pole Inn.

'You really should be hospitalised,' the doctor went on.

'But, given where you live, I think you should stay at home and rest.'

Take it easy, were the doctor's parting words. He was a caring and practical man. A doctor whose judgement we trusted. But, as he had never had a reason to visit us at home, he obviously had no idea what winter was like with us. Tomintoul was bad enough, the Braes were even worse, but Corrunich was positively arctic. Ice, icicles and deep drifts. Exposed and freezing. In order to get to the phone box, Jonathan had had to plod through the wind-driven snow in poor visibility. Chilled and in pain. He still had to plod all the way back. For the second time that day.

It was snowing heavily when we approached Norman's farm. We had difficulty seeing through the barrage of snow hitting the windscreen. The wipers couldn't clear it away fast enough. We had been shopping for supplies again. We always went together as we had no way of contacting each other if anything were to happen. Besides, we could usually get the shopping home in one go if we both carried it. So the car was full of cumbersome supplies and, reluctantly, we had come to ask Norman if we could drive it through his fields to get a little closer to our home. We would then only have to trek across the moor for quarter of a mile. Which was about all Jonathan's healing bottom could bear. As we slipped and skidded towards his fields, we could just make out Norman's figure loading hay into a trailer, directly ahead of us. There he was, this hardy highlander, outside in just a torn, checked shirt and an open, battered jacket. And, of course, his hat.

'Aye, please yourself,' he growled at our request to use his fields.

He wasn't being unfriendly, it was just that time of the day. He was busy. And he had had a hard night. His blood-shot eyes revealed just how hard.

'Keep the speed up,' he shouted, as he kicked open the gate for us.

We waved thanks and kept going. *Come on, come on*, we chanted, encouraging the car to charge the distance and ride the bumps. We had no sense of our surroundings, just the sound of the straining engine as it lurched through the sea of snow. It was vital to keep the momentum going. If we stopped, we would sink. *Come on, you can do it*, we said, patting the dashboard. *Thump*. The engine cut out. We were stuck.

We got out of the car prepared to shovel it free but the front wheels were firmly wedged in a deep hole that had been concealed by the snow. We took it in turns to push, rocking it backwards and forwards, but the car would not budge. This was exactly what we had hoped wouldn't happen. We looked at each other in despair. We must have looked a sorry sight when our burly knight appeared in his old, groaning tractor pulling the trailer of hay. Somewhere in the exposed field there were animals to feed.

Taking advantage of the meagre shelter in his battered cab, Norman stuffed some tobacco into his pipe and struck a match. With his pipe successfully lit, he stepped down to join us and leaned heavily on our car. He drew on his pipe and, casually, started to chat. We couldn't believe it. Propelled by an increasingly fierce wind, the snow was slapping into us from all directions. In spite of our woolly fleeces, we were shivering with cold but Norman was standing in this freezing squall in clothing fit for a Scottish summer, with only his shaggy beard and spirit in his belly for warmth. *And he wanted to chat!* While our car was, ignominiously, stuck in a hole.

Obvious though it was, we reminded him of our predicament. It seemed churlish to point it out but we weren't one hundred per cent sure that he had even noticed. He got the message and slowly lifted his weight off the car and began to prod the snow with his crook, leisurely circumnavigating the scene.

'Put it in tae reverse,' he barked. 'And I'll give it a push.'

Jonathan eased his tender, aching bum into the driving seat while Norman crouched at the front of the car. I joined him and pushed with all my might. *Whey hey!* The wheels raised out of the hole. For a moment. Then they slipped back in. Norman grunted and crouched lower. We pushed and heaved again. *Whey hey again!* The front of the car raised into the air and the car moved backwards. I was still pushing. *Whoaaah!* And fell flat on my face. Norman, who had tumbled on to his knees, picked himself up and tried, in vain, to re-light his pipe. He looked calm for a man who, with seemingly little effort, had single-handedly lifted the car out of the hole.

'Must be the whisky,' I said, congratulating him.

'Aye,' he agreed with a twinkle in his eye. 'It's bloody good stuff.'

'Ach, you didn't have to do that,' Norman mumbled with a grin that belied his words. He was clearly delighted. A highlander never says no to a bottle of whisky. It was our way of showing that we had appreciated his help with the car.

'We thought you could use the container for biscuits afterwards,' I said, pointing to the cylindrical tin that contained the bottle.

'Ah ha,' he chuckled, not missing a beat. 'You're a Scot for sure.'

We had to use Norman's fields one more time that winter. After weeks without electricity, our generator was finally fixed. It had taken a long time to get the spare parts. All the way from Italy. But now its heavy, cumbersome body was weighing down the back of the car and we had to get it home. There was no way we could get the car up the track, which was still fully entrenched with three-foot snow-drifts and, after the last effort, we were less than keen to physically drag the generator up. However, we didn't feel comfortable about asking Norman if we could use his fields. We didn't like taking liberties. But, on the other hand, if we didn't get the generator home then, we would have to wait until the snow thawed on the track. Sometime in the spring. And that was too long as, apart from the lack of lights, music and the use of the computer, we were feeling the cold. The gravity-fed central heating was working but the radiators were barely warm. We needed power to pump the water through the pipes to take the chill and damp out of the old lady. So it was with mixed feelings that we knocked on Norman's back door.

'You're lucky, you just *bide* here,' shouted Jean over the cacophony of seven dogs and a menagerie of geese, hens, cats and a calf that hung around the doorway.

Jean was Norman's *bidie'in*. It had taken some time to learn her name but now we were sure to never forget it. Tough but shy Jean. With lively green eyes and a kind smile. Welsh in origin but sounded as if she was from the Braes. She fitted in so well. But then she'd have to, to live with Norman. In the Braes.

'They used to have to suck the blood of their animals to survive,' she said, referring to the crofters who once inhabited the glen. They did more than 'bide', they had to live off the land. 'The animals would be so weak by the end of the winter they would have to carry each one out to pasture.'

And with that she gave us the green light to proceed through the snow in our modern Japanese vehicle, which was laden with an Italian generator and a few Safeway bags stuffed full of produce that those crofters would never even have heard of.

'The tomatoes must have fallen out on the track,' I said, as I searched once more through the shopping.

We had been shopping again and we had just walked up through a filthy blizzard with our habitual bundle of supermarket bags. Most of the heavy articles, like the tins of dog food, had been stuffed into backpacks but the other things had remained in plastic bags. For the long trek, we had tried to double-bag everything but we had obviously slipped up with one of the bags containing vegetables as it had burst at the bottom corner and the tomatoes were now missing. Seemingly, a cucumber had conveniently lodged itself across the bottom thus barring the escape of any other vegetables.

It wasn't the first time we had lost shopping on the track and sometimes we did go back to find it but, on this night, it would have been madness. The wind was coming in sideways from the north, hitting every inch of exposed flesh with hard, stinging sleet. There was no mercy as the storm slapped into us, practically knocking us over, so that we took useless steps to the side, rather like a horse in a dressage event. It took a lot of effort to control the swinging bags and steer a direct course. With heads down to protect our eyes, we just concentrated on getting home as our boots plodded, methodically, on through the snow and ice. Two steps forwards and one to side. The visibility was so poor, we had no idea how much distance we had covered and we had to use the fences, when we bumped into them, as a guide. It was only when we bumped into a fence that we knew shouldn't have been there that we realised we had walked right past Corrunich.

'No, they're definitely not here,' I said, having emptied all the shopping out.

'Well, I'm not going back out for them tonight,'

Jonathan said adamantly. The night was too wild. He would look for them tomorrow on his way down to the phone box. They would be frozen by then but they weren't important enough to risk getting lost in the blizzard. However, if it had been a ripe lump of creamy gorgonzola that had fallen out, he might not have been so adamant.

On clear nights the winter skies were spectacular. But nothing prepared us for our first glimpse of the *aurora borealis*, the northern lights. We had just eaten the most beautifully tender medallions of wild venison fillet and were wiping chunks of bread around our plates to soak up the last smidgeons of whisky and juniper gravy when we were plunged into darkness. In our greed, we had forgotten the generator. It had run out of fuel. As it needed to be filled every five hours, it was a common and tedious occurrence that required one of us, usually Jonathan, to take the diesel bucket from the barn to the fuel tank by the gate, fill it up, and then return to the barn to fill up the generator. A simple enough task in daylight but at night it had to be done by torchlight. Occasionally, to make it easier, we both did it at night. One to hold the torch while the other filled the bucket and generator. Occasionally, we both did it to keep each other company as we often got spooked by unidentified creaks and rustles from deep within the dark, hollow barn. Bats, mice, wood pigeons. And creatures of the imagination.

On this particular night of supreme indulgence, without

the aid of a television and with only each other for company, we had allowed our imaginations to run amok and scared ourselves silly with frightening stories. Like everybody else, we had both seen *The Shining*. Needless to say, we stepped out into the night together. And there they were in their full glory. Great rainbow-coloured beams projecting from the base of the northern horizon into the clear sky, sweeping across it like huge, theatre spotlights. A mesmerising sight. The conditions were perfect. Silent. Still. Cold. And, above all, no phantom axe murderers to be seen.

On the crisp, clear winter days I loved walking in the hills. With the solid snow squeaking and crunching under my mountain boots, the frozen white surface giving me the pleasurable sensation that I was taller than I was. I would sit in a sheltered, hilltop peat bog and lose myself in the silent view of Ben Avon and Lochnagar, sharing a juicy orange with Biglie who, panting excitedly, was quite relieved to have a short break from chasing the white hares. Powered by long hind legs that projected them up vertical slopes with ease, the hares were usually too fast. But, there were times when he did catch one. A dog with a killer instinct but no need to kill, he would toy with his prey and guard it with a snarl if I approached. As I continued to walk, he would dig in the snow and tuck the hare under a juniper bush or in a clump of heather, cover it up, and leave it behind. A kind of burial ritual. But it seemed such a senseless death. So I decided that, depending on the state of the kill, either we or he should eat it.

Once Biglie had carried the first floppy, dead hare home, the difficult part was extracting it from his mouth. The wild origins of this soppy dog raced to the surface. He had wolf in his eyes and wolf in his bared sharp teeth, his deep growling stating proprietorship. After a certain amount of bullying and bribing, the hare was reluctantly dropped to the ground and he hungrily positioned himself to watch what we were going to do with it. This was the part neither of us was looking forward to. Skinning and gutting. With long, tuggable ears and big, brown eyes, the hare looked soft and cuddly. A character in children's stories. Some people even compare the skinning of rabbits and hares to slipping off a baby's sleep-suit. Keen to remove the focus of sentiment, Jonathan lopped off the head. Then he could concentrate on supper. Casseroled with pears and ale.

Alan and Dalla turned up, out of the blue. On foot. I was making porridge. Lost in a reverie of porridge on safari. A red dawn rising above the thorn trees on the dry African plains or the wet morning mist lifting over the clearing in a dense, damp forest. Giant mounds of fresh elephant and buffalo dung still steaming in the cool air around our tents. Wherever we camped in the bush, my father always made porridge for breakfast. Once a Scot, always a Scot. And for a Scot, whose primary role was to set up the first medical school in Nairobi, the duty of porridge-maker was therapy. It had to be made just right. With a little salt to bring out the taste. And, if there was no milk, we would eat it with butter or syrup, both of which would melt in the steaming porridge. But, back in Scotland, in the comfort of his home, my father prefers the traditional method of porridge in one bowl and the milk in another, dipping his spoon of hot porridge into the cold milk, so the two never mingle. It's funny how something so simple can be so complex. Some people eat porridge with milk and sugar, some with milk and no sugar, others insist on just salt, and then there's the old-fashioned porridge made with pin-head oatmeal which gives it a chewy, nutty texture, the taste reminiscent of popcorn. But there's nothing like the smell of freshly-made porridge in the open air or on cold mornings. And that morning at Corrunich it was porridge weather. Sombre and cold. As if no light would come through the sky that day. The kind of day you lace your porridge with a dram.

The knock at the back door made my attention jump back from the bush to the cold-looking figures of Alan and Dalla in snow-covered boots. What a surprise. As the new guardians of Corrunich, we had given them an open invitation to come back and see us. But we had expected some warning. Apparently, they had sent one but it had been sitting in our post-box at the end of the track. And, of course, we hadn't been to collect the post for days.

'We had hoped you would have got our letter,' said Alan, grinning as he handed over the mail. 'But I see it's been sitting in your box.'

I opened the letter and read it with mild trepidation. Not sure if they had come all this way for a cup of tea or a week. A couple of nights, it said. No problem. And from a pocket, they produced a bottle of whisky. My thoughts immediately went to our supplies. We were a bit low. Lots of porridge and whisky though. And some onions, garlic, eggs, a tin of tomatoes and a few sad-looking peppers, their skins as wrinkled as an elephant's hide. *Menemen*. That's what we could have. Simple Turkish bus-station food. Ideal for a tasty impromptu meal. I would bake bread to mop it up and there were enough eggs for pancakes too. Buckwheat pancakes drizzled with purple syrup made from plump blaeberries I had picked in the hills at the end of August. But that was it. I had no idea what we would have the next day. Perhaps Biglie would catch a hare.

Once we were on our own again, with all the chores done, I set off up the hill with Biglie. I needed to reclaim my space after having people to stay. It was a little too late in the afternoon to go far as the sky was growing dark so I headed for a flat ridge we call the saddle. It was hard going as the snow was thigh deep in parts and the sky started throwing icy pellets into my face. Then just as I reached the saddle an almighty blizzard blasted out of the heavens above. It was so heavy, I could barely see beyond my nose. And when I called for Biglie my voice trailed off pathetically in the wind. Trying not to panic, I surged forward in what I guessed was the direction of our cottage and sank. Up to my waist. I knew I was in one of the saddle's many peat pools which, lined with boggy peat and moss, were knee to thigh deep at the best of times but, on this tempestuous day, they were plugged with a thick layer of snow. Frantically, I tried to get out. My boots were stuck in the toffee-like bog below. Again, I called for Biglie. Still, he didn't come. Oh no, poor boy, I thought. I suddenly had visions of him stuck in a hole too, his front legs hopelessly scrabbling at the snow in a desperate attempt to pull himself out. Panic began to set in. These highland hills were notorious for claiming lives every year and I didn't want to add to the statistics. Not here. Not so ridiculously close to home. What a stupid mistake. I could have been at home now, curled up in front of the fire. Instead, I would freeze if I didn't get out of this hole now. The tears began to trickle down my cheeks. It was hopeless. There was nothing to grip on to.

Biglie rolled into me, slapping snow into my face. He was wriggling on his back with all four paws in the air, making a sort of happy gurgling sound. He loved the snow. He loved blizzards. He was panting, which probably meant he had been chasing hares all over the saddle, using his nose as a compass. And then he got up on his feet and bounced up and down, thinking this was a game. Half of me was in a hole and my head was at the right height for sniffing and licking. I was so relieved to see him that I grabbed hold of his solid, muscular body and gave him a hug. He flipped over on to the snow and rolled into me again, tunnelling his nose through the snow. Which gave me an idea and I started digging with my hands under his nose. Being a dog, he thought there must be something there. Why else would I be digging? So he dug too. With much more speed and success. Until he had dug away enough for me to lean into and get some elbow leverage. Then with a great deal of kicking and cursing, I heaved my soaking lower torso out of the snow and bog and, once again, headed in what I thought was the direction of home. Only this time I walked gingerly, with my feet squelching in their soggy boots, keeping Biglie by my side as the light faded around us. When we reached the back door, it was pitch dark.

'I feel like Scott of the Antarctic,' said our friend David Allison, the guitar-playing journalist from the BBC. He shook the snow out of his musician's bush of hair.

He and his wife, Sab, had just walked all the way from the bottom of the track. He in a leather jacket and a pair of trainers, she in funky, yellow plastic boots and a fashionable bag hanging off her shoulder. He's more comfortable plucking his strings in the clubs and festivals of Europe's cities. She is Californian. They had never been in weather like it.

'Just a mild storm,' we teased.

Still out of breath, David sat down. In the elated way of someone who has just come through a dramatic experience, he recounted the moments he had felt like man pitted against the elements. The moments they had sunk deep into the snow, the moments they couldn't even see where they were going. The moments when Sab had thought she was going to die. She giggled at the memory as she busily peeled off her soaked layers, pulling her fingers through her long, snow-speckled locks. We made some hot tea and pushed them through to the warm birch fire in the sitting-room.

'This is the life,' Sab chirped in her sunny accent, tucking into her third piece of sticky, buttered home-made gingerbread in between applications of ruby lipstick to her lips. She was so close to the flames, she was practically on fire.

Indeed, the life that first winter was fairly idyllic. Simple and solitary. Time to think and reflect. Our days were spent organising our living. There was wood to be chopped, bread to be baked, yoghurt to be fermented and set, and a basic village cheese to be made, which we ate with a winter jam made from dried figs and pine nuts for breakfast. There was always the washing to do which, once it was hung out on the line, froze solid. When I brought it in it stood upright in the bath. Then there was the continual fixing and filling of the generator, digging the car out of the snow, walking up and down the track for mail and supplies and, at the end of the day, a bottle of red wine, a lively game of backgammon, and a deliciously deep hot bath in candlelight. We had no television and no phone. No bills to pay. No real contact with the outside world. If people wanted to contact us, they had to write. Even then, we didn't always collect the mail. It was the kind of life a lot of people dream of having for a short period of time. A moment of catharsis. A fast from reality. But not once did we take it for granted. We were too afraid of losing it all.

In the middle of April we would be celebrating our first anniversary at Corrunich. It would be like reaching the crossover point, when the dream became reality. We had been in our remote outpost for one whole year and we had little to show for it. Our new business plan proved that, given the amount we would have to borrow, the photography workshops would only be viable if they were filled every week of the year. That alone would have been a tall order but the severity of the current winter deemed that it would also be impossible. So we were stumped and broke. But we weren't about to give up. The spirit of Corrunich had got under our skin. Instead, to give ourselves more time, we arranged for a capital release on our property and, for a few days a week, Jonathan returned to Edinburgh to stay with our friends Alex and Anne Caroline while he worked at the Scotch Malt Whisky Society. I stayed at home and clung on to our dreams.

Biglie protected me in Jonathan's absence. If I embarked on something that excluded him, like cursing the generator as I tried to crankstart it, he would sit by the fence and keep watch, his ears rising and falling with alertness. No sound escaped him. I hadn't been so well guarded since I was a child when my protector had been a Masai warrior. Naked, but for a *shuka* (a cloth hung over one shoulder), he had stood silently by me with his long, lethal spear. As I idly attributed Biglie with human qualities, I decided that in another life he too would have been a Masai warrior. With a Ph.D. For in addition to his noble poise and sleek coat, his indisputable fearlessness and hunting skills, he was good company and understood everything I said.

But, in spite of the companionship of my canine friend, Jonathan's vociferous presence was sorely missed. This was not how it was meant to be. We had to find a way of staying here. Together. We still believed that, sometime in the future, we would set up the photography workshops but, for the time being, we would have to try and make a living from freelance work. Jonathan could complete some of the projects he was working on in the bathroom, where he spent hours in the dark developing and printing his black-and-white work. He loved the smell of the chemicals and the magic of the print coming to life. If it wasn't for the cramped space and lack of ventilation, he could have been in heaven. I was much more keen on using the bathroom for bathing but, in my own way, I could try to create work too. Surely, I thought, I could pull from something I had done. Ski instructing was too seasonal and, anyway, the season was almost over, teaching English as a foreign language was out of the question so I would have to pull from journalism or publishing, the other two areas I had worked in. Or cooking. And so, once again, a dreamer to the core, albeit at times a realistic one, I blew the dust off a typescript we had been carrying around with us for a few years, along with a file full of rejection letters.

The script, which had been lovingly typed out on the old Underwood we had bought in Ohio, was for a cookery book. Turkish food to be exact. A subject I knew something about as I had written food and restaurant reviews in

Turkey but also a subject in which we had a vested interest. It was the food we loved and ate at home. Several years before, we had presented the book to a large publishing house in New York. We had even cooked food to take to the meeting but the editors, who between mouthfuls raved about the recipes, were not keen on the association with Turkey. It would be a marketing bomb, they stressed. The Middle East, and that included Turkey, was not America's favourite place at that moment. The Iran-Contra and hostage taking in Lebanon were foremost in people's minds. If the food was good, they had argued, the origin wasn't that important. Anyway, what was the difference between Turkish and Greek food? They could use the recipes and jazz them up with descriptive titles using words like 'zany' and 'wacky'. That way people would buy the book. But we held on to it. No better off, but our integrity in tact. The fact that the recipes were Turkish was the whole point. It was a fascinating food culture with wide-ranging culinary influences. Obviously, we hadn't made that clear. We had to create an argument, fighting for its right to be published and stand alongside the books on Greek and Middle Eastern food. And then rewrite it on disk and target publishers in London.

A great deal of research had gone into the book, including several, at times dangerous, forays into bandit country in the east of Turkey. In search of a divine hot hummus, I had been chased by knife-wielding gypsies through their encampment above Lake Van. At the wheel of the car was my Turkish colleague and friend, Kenan, who with his

Winter at Corrunich

Ghillie as a young
girl in Kenya

Ghillie's family home
in Kenya

Jonathan as a young boy in the waterfront garden of the yalı

Jonathan's family yalı in Istanbul

Corrunich looking jolly in the summer

Remote and snowbound

Jonathan pulling the gas cylinder

Jonathan working on the generator

Stuck in a snowdrift

Friends at last –
Biglie and Aslan lie
in the sun

Yasmin and Zeki
playing in the
stream

Ghillie and Biglie
sliding off the roof

Out for a walk with
Zeki in the overland
pram

Ghillie and
Jonathan with a
baby Yasmin in
backpack (© Claire
Hartley)

Yasmin going to school

The family

quick thinking had already got us out of many sticky situations but, on this occasion, he had struggled as the tiny Skoda skidded and spun in the sand. Fierce dogs leaped at our windows as the gypsies tried to catch up with the car which suddenly, just in the nick of time, gained momentum and sped onwards out of trouble. On one dark night when the stars were shooting down from the sky, Kenan's knowledge of Kurdish, which he had learnt when he was sent to teach in a Kurdish village for a year as punishment for hitting an officer during his military service, literally saved our hides. A Kurd we had given a lift to advised us to leave the route we were on. It was too dangerous, he warned. The PKK (Kurdish Separatist Movement) would be setting up road blocks which were notorious for the lack of mercy shown. Money and camera equipment were just the booty; several tourists lost their lives. The next day our detour took us through a hilltop settlement where the women were washing clothes in the fast-flowing rivulets and a group of children were playing nearby. We stopped and I stupidly raised my camera. Like bats out of hell, the children surrounded us, reaching in through the open windows trying to grab anything they could. The tape deck, tapes, sunglasses, map, film, the camera, and my earrings which were dangling from my ears. It all happened so fast. Hungry faces, dirty teeth, spiky hair and grabbing hands. 'Drive!' screamed Kenan, desperately trying to roll up his window. Slapping away the hands that were pulling at my ears, I shoved the gear-stick forwards and roared off in first gear. The relief on Kenan's face spoke volumes.

The children wouldn't have stopped and there would have been hungry adults close behind. We had heard the stories.

Our brief brush with the uglier side of life was swept away by the warm, spontaneous hospitality of a postman in Kars. We were strangers to him but he invited us to his home for the night. He woke up his wife and family and they gave us glasses of strong tea and bread with a pungent, crumbly cheese that had been maturing underground in an earthenware pot for two years. Then he told us we should get some sleep and laid out the mattresses we had all been sitting on. I was led outside by his daughter who held a candle to light the way down the lane to the communal loo. She made clicking noises with her tongue to frighten the rats and then opened the wooden door to show me the deep hole in the ground. I peed in total darkness, praying that nothing would nip my bum. Back inside, our host bid us goodnight and then he and his family squeezed into the only other room, where they usually ate. The cocks woke us up at first light and Kenan and I took it in turns to use the hole in the ground, which I was glad I hadn't seen the night before. Baked by the morning sun, the stench was the first thing that hit me, then the flies, and lastly the cockroaches. The hole was moving and so was the ground around it. I clenched my pelvic floor tightly and resigned myself to waiting for a bush once we were on the road again. On our return, we were given a bucket of water to wash in before our host took us into the room that he and his family had slept in. There laid out on a wide, round tray was our breakfast. Fresh eggs, more pungent cheese, bread and the local honey, made from poppy pollen, which was fiery and mildly hallucinogenic. We sat on the floor and tucked in, while the host drank tea and chatted to us and his family huddled in the doorway, watching. It was moments like this that made travelling so humbling. People with nothing, so willing to share everything. In Britain, we have no idea what hospitality really is. We offer it with conditions. In Turkey it flows through the veins. I may never see that postman again but he and others like him, who shared a slice of their lives with me, contributed to the whole love affair I had with Turkey and I, in turn, wanted to share that with others. And, always, at the root of such hospitality there is food. So Jonathan and I tried to breathe some life into the old typescript, to give a feeling for the food and the culture – as they go hand in hand – and to make it engaging for the interested traveller and cook.

At the same time as our first year at Corrunich came to a close, our Subaru came to an unjust end. Not far from Balmoral Castle. We had just entered the twisty, single-track road that leads over the hills to Tomintoul when a car, descending too fast around the blind turns, crashed into us. In an attempt to get out of the way, we had pulled into a narrow passing place but the car swung too widely around the bend and hit the driving side. The bonnet crumpled, trapping the front wheels. A complete write-off. We had been heading home from a visit to my parents in

Braemar but now we had no choice but to go back there. The oncoming car, containing two skiers in a rush to get back to Fife, was only mildly dented. They were unapologetic but agreed to give us a lift into Braemar.

While my mother made us cups of soothing hot tea, my father offered to lend us his Land Rover. I was amazed that he was willing to part with it, even temporarily, as apart from the fact that it was his pride and joy, the last time I had been at the wheel of his Land Rover I had driven it into a tree. It was, of course, a different Land Rover and I was only eight years old at the time but I had, undeniably, driven into a tree. The only tree, runs the family joke, in the Serengeti Plains. I had been driving off road, fondly termed *bundu bashing* by white settlers, while my father filmed the migration from the passenger seat. My brother, with whom I took it in turns to drive, was sitting in the back leaning out of the window, watching the game. I, on the other hand, was supposed to be weaving in and out of thorn bushes, ant-eater holes, large boulders, and hyena lairs but, alas, I must have been distracted by the baying and grunting of hundreds of wildebeast, kongoni, giraffe, zebra, and Thomson's gazelle as they moved through the hazy heat, kicking up the dust. Or perhaps I was just keeping an eye on the hungry predators lingering on the edge of the migrating column, seeking the moment to attack and kill the weak, the young, and vulnerable. What none of us had envisaged when we had left the remote Ndutu Lodge earlier that morning was that the three of us would be the most vulnerable of all, returning to the lodge on foot with only a *panga* (a large knife) for defence.

Back in the Braes, we were treated with a new deference. People we didn't even know waved to us. Farmers and keepers stopped to chat. It was the old Land Rover, of course. Series three. Good condition. They all wanted to know how much we had paid for it.

I was reminded of the reaction my mother got when, with a headscarf tied under her chin, she used to drive along the Deeside road to the local hairdresser. School children, tourists, and people in their gardens would stop what they were doing and wave. Even policemen would stand at the roadside and salute. They had mistaken her for the Queen who, at that time, with a headscarf holding her hair in place, often drove freely around the area in her Land Rover.

Towards the end of April, the radio was tuned to talk of spring flowers and sunshine. Apparently, it was a fine day in London. A touch of summer had hit the streets. People were strolling in the parks in their shorts. And Jonathan's mother and aunt, dressed in light clothing, were packing the car for their journey north. They were to be with us late that evening. That was the intention. Later than planned they crossed the border into Scotland. Into gloom. The further north they got, the weather closed in, dark and menacing. Up the steep Satan's Slide, which used to be curved and called Devil's Elbow, and on to the

Glenshee summit, they found themselves caught in a white-out. They just managed to make it to Braemar and checked into a hotel. At two in the morning.

Meanwhile, we were in the midst of a full-blown blizzard. An arctic squall had descended on us yet again. We spent the day cleaning the cottage, making up the beds and warming them with hot water bottles, chopping wood and stoking the fire, baking bread and making soup. By late evening, we were glued to the window looking out for a torchlight on the horizon. They couldn't phone but they knew the drill. They would leave the car at the bottom of the track, put on boots and warm clothes, and walk up. As soon as we spotted the tiny dot of torchlight coming over the hill, we would come out to meet them and help them with their luggage. We had listened anxiously to the weather updates on the fierce gales and heavy snow and were relieved at the absence of any accident reports. Eventually, we flopped into bed in the early hours of the morning, leaving the generator on so that, in the unlikely event that they would arrive during the night, the lit up windows would guide them to the cottage. Without a phone there was nothing else we could do until the morning.

We woke up to a striking calm. Like a painting. Land and sky seemed to melt into one another. Milky white. Motionless and silent. And, once again, the fine snow had found its way into our loft and back porch. Still hoping that Jonathan's mother and aunt would turn up, we tried to carry on as normal, digging our way out of the back door and emptying the loft before the melting snow dripped down the walls and all over the landing. With no sign of the two ladies by eleven o'clock, the worry overwhelmed us and Jonathan elected to trudge the miles to the phone box. First, he would call the police for a road and accident report. Then he would call my parents in Braemar. It was just possible that his mother, unable to reach us, might have called them. My mother answered the phone in a chipper mood. She was in the throws of a lunch party, and, yes, his mother and aunt were there, in the sitting-room with the other guests. They would be on their way sometime in the afternoon after lunch. It was certainly a relief to know they were safe and comfortable but, after all our worrying, we were a bit annoyed at how unconcerned everyone else seemed to be.

We waited in that useless way when you know people are going to arrive but have no idea when, so you don't do anything constructive. At about four o'clock that afternoon, two empty-handed figures, moving slowly over the hill, caught our attention. We headed out to meet them in the full knowledge that later we would have to go all the way to the bottom of the track to get their luggage. On seeing us, Jonathan's aunt, sensibly dressed in a raincoat and wellington boots, strode across the moor. But his mother sank through the soft snow into a deep hole and almost disappeared from view. We rushed over to find her lying in the snow laughing, dressed in a little pink mini-skirt under a fur coat. Gently reproving her attire, Jonathan reached under her arms and heaved her out of the hole leaving her wellington boots behind. At least she was wearing boots this time. But, not surprisingly, she was chilled and had to be helped across the moor into the warmth of the kitchen.

A little while later, with their luggage brought up from the car for them and resuscitated with cups of hot tea, the two ladies sat in front of a roaring birch fire. 'You know, I could live here,' Jonathan's aunt announced suddenly, with great enthusiasm. 'It would be easy really. All you need is a stock of dried beans.' This was from a lady who had spent many years in the heat of India. With servants. Jonathan and I looked at each other with knowing smiles. *We must be making it look too easy!*

Two days later, when the weather brightened and the snow began to melt, the ponies came back on to the land around Corrunich. It was to be a short stay as the ranger and his wife were about to move from the area. The ponies had been kept lower down all winter and, as we hadn't been expecting them, our gate was still open when they raced over to their favourite haunt. The washing-line. Where the clothes were thawing out. Frozen, like stiff sheets of cardboard, they had been hanging there for two days. Before I could stop him, the stallion was at the back door and gave Jonathan's mother, who was just stepping outside to have a cigarette, such a fright that she shot back into the safety of the kitchen.

While Biglie danced noisily around his big friend, I chopped up some apples to try and bribe the stallion towards the gate. Jonathan's aunt plucked up the courage to help me and together we managed to coax him around to the front of the cottage, about ten metres from the gate, when he caught sight of his handsome reflection in the sitting-room window. *Another stallion!* He tried to charge it. Jonathan's mother, who was now smoking in the sitting-room, held a blanket over the window thinking it would block out the reflection but it only served to enhance it. Confused, the stallion snorted and chased Jonathan's aunt who, in a panic, dropped her tray of apples and made a mad dash for the back door. Two down, and neither of the ladies willing to emerge again, I was left to tackle the stallion alone. A frisky chap, the leader of his equine gang, and charged up by the threat of another stallion. I wasn't sure I would be able to handle him on my own. He only ever seemed to respond to the ranger's wife. I had often watched him chase the ranger himself. It was like a game. The stallion would chase and the ranger would run, staggering over the uneven ground to the safety of the gate. But, thankfully, help was on its way. Trudging methodically across the moor through the snow, Jonathan was dragging a large, red torpedo, the gas cylinder for the hot water which had run out again. And together, with one of us coaxing him from the front and the other gently thumping his rump, we managed to encourage the stubborn stallion out of our gate.

When we got to the bottom of the track, we were surprised that the daffodils were in bud and the trees and road were wet with rain. A drop of a few hundred feet and it was a different season. At 1,500ft, Corrunich was still in the throws of a snowy winter. We had walked down to the car in Gore-Tex jackets, mountain boots and gaiters and there, standing by our post-box, sticking his thumb out to request a lift, was a young man dressed in a dirty, over-sized jacket and ripped jeans. He was unkempt looking with long, greasy hair. Scruffy in a city way. Definitely, a stranger to the Braes.

'Are you going to the village?' the young man asked in an Australian accent.

'Will Tomintoul do?'

'Yeah, I need a bath,' he explained.

Like many Australians he had travelled half-way around the world to their Mecca: London. And unlike many Londoners, he had hitched all the way north, over the border, to the Braes of Glenlivet. To stay by himself in a friend's holiday cottage for a week. But he had no hot water. There was plenty of water in the tank, including a dead sheep, but nothing to heat it with. So he needed to get a gas tube. We knew the problem, we sympathised. And briefly described where we lived.

'You must be the Spanish photographer,' he said, turning to Jonathan.

Spanish, Turkish, whatever. Once locals know you're a foreigner, that's exactly what you are. A foreigner. They're not that interested in the nationality. As long as you're not English. And even that is generally treated in good humour in this area. The locals tend to take people as they come. If you're friendly, they're friendly. But if an Englishman squeezes a highlander too hard, a history of resentment can come to the fore. Everyone draws their own highland line, some say it's Deeside, others say it's Perth, and if you come from below that line, you're a 'southerner'. Foreigners, on the other hand, present no real threat. And this Australian, whose ancestors may even have been Scottish, had been drinking at a very highland pub, the Pole Inn, where he heard that a Spanish photographer lived somewhere deep in the hills. And never came out.

'That must be someone else,' Jonathan said, wickedly widening the scope, remembering that Alan and Dalla, both of whom were English, had told us that they used to go to the Pole Inn to find out what they had been doing all week. The stories used to surprise them.

'So how are you today?' Jonathan asked Norman, whose winter growth was so bushy he looked like he'd eaten a bear for breakfast, the tufts of hair still stuck to his face.

We were standing in knee-deep mud and melting, porridge-like snow, the last vestiges of a slow and straggly transition from winter to spring. There were moments of charm – creamy skies about to explode with a passing snow shower, wind-driven rain that looked like curtains of chainmail streaking across the sky, and the early morning frost encasing the long grasses in giant ice popsicles. But, for the most part, the stale snow was draining off the hills leaving them bare and patchy. And the ground soggy.

Grimacing, Norman looked up at the sky for a moment, then down at the ground, and then into the distance. Then his grimace slipped into a smile. A blackened smile. The long, cold winter nights of whisky and tobacco seemed to have taken a toll on his teeth too. He fumbled in his pocket for a match and lit his pipe. He took several slow, methodical puffs, maximising the time he always seemed to have. The time one needed to calmly digest a bear. Finally, he removed the pipe from his mouth and let out a big sigh.

'Clouds, snow, mud, wet,' he summed up, succinctly. 'That's how I am today.'

The winter season was coming to an end.

Making A Living

'So, have you been away south all winter?' asked the younger and chattier of the two farmers.

For six months no one had passed Corrunich. For six months no vehicle had been able to get up the track. Now that the snow had almost gone, the first was an old Land Rover. Just two old boys taking a drive. Through the hills with a bottle of whisky.

'No,' we replied, indignantly. 'We've been here all the time.'

'Oh?' he uttered, looking genuinely surprised. 'I didn't know anyone stayed here in winter. I thought you would have gone back home.'

'This *is* our home,' I pointed out. 'Our only home.'

'Are you nae English then?'

We shook our heads. No, Scottish and Turkish, we explained. Not that we felt strongly about either identity. Like many of our generation who have had the good fortune to travel we felt more international really but that wouldn't have been a satisfactory answer. Just pretentious.

'Ach, that's all right then,' they both assured us, beaming with drunken pleasure. And stuck out their big, leathery hands to introduce themselves. One of them was a Macdonald. The last in a line that had farmed in Glenlivet since fleeing from the Jacobites in 1745.

'What do you want to live out here for?' the driver of the tanker asked acridly. It was a foul day. Mist. Driving sleet. And bitterly cold. After the long winter, our fuel tanks were completely empty so we couldn't fill the generator and the heating had gone off. The old lady was beginning to feel damp and cold again.

'You should have seen it a couple of weeks ago,' Jonathan said, making conversation. 'The snow was over the fences.'

'What a God-forsaken place,' the driver droned on, as if he hadn't heard. Rapidly distancing himself from any semblance of manners. 'You won't get me back out here, I can assure you.'

Fortunately, he wasn't the regular driver.

Ceremoniously, we dumped about forty bags of rubbish at the bottom of our track. The accumulation of a snow-bound winter. Including persistent reminders for a television licence and council tax. With no access, no phone, no television, no electricity, and no rubbish collection in the winter, we had felt the official bodies concerned were more than welcome to walk up and check. Preferably on a stormy day.

We also tried to clear up some of Norman's winter rubbish. Black, white and yellow feed bags. In the storms, they had blown all over the place. Hooked on to the barbed-wire fencing, wrapped around trees in the woods, poking out of patches of persistent snow, and semi-submerged in puddles on the track. The mess didn't seem to bother Norman. Would he mind if I picked up all the bags, I had asked him in a ridiculously polite way. Please yourself, he had replied, amused. But the accumulation of bags didn't stop. Every time he fed the animals, the emptied bags continued to blow out of his tractor and trailer and roll across the fields. Picking them up seemed like a pointless exercise until, as we were driving along the track one day, I saw Norman collecting them in a bundle. Could he really be tidying up his own litter? We stopped beside him to chat. As we always do. 'These any use to you?' he asked sincerely, holding out the bundle of ripped, muddy bags as if they genuinely served a purpose. Or, at least, he believed we thought they did. What could we say? We didn't want to offend him so, like grateful idiots, we took them on board. A bundle of useless bags that we would have to bin or burn.

Jonathan was in the barn with the generator in pieces. It had packed in again. He was in such a foul mood, I was keeping out of his way, standing at the kitchen window looking through the binoculars. There were curlews nesting on the moor and two people had just appeared over by Norman's gate. Both had got my attention. The curlews with their long curved beaks were gracefully wandering around on the peaceful moor but the two people, who I guessed were walkers, the first walkers of the season, were hovering around the gate, bobbing up and down in a most unusual manner. I focused the binoculars on them. A big pair of squatting pink buttocks zoomed into vision. The first buttocks of the season. It served me right for being so nosy but, with a wood directly behind her, she could have picked a less conspicuous spot. Like most people though, without the sound of the generator or any sign of life, she must have assumed that no one lived in our remote cottage.

'I see you had people on your roof today,' Hamish said, pouring a drop of murky water into his dram. His water supply was running clearer. No frogs in it that day.

Ladderfoot had become our regular watering hole. A sophisticated watering hole. Only half a mile along the track, closer if we took a direct route through the reedy marshes, so we walked to it. And, in the winter, Hamish and Pam had to walk to it too. Now it was May, the first time that year that they had managed to get their old Range Rover all the way to the cottage, so we were treated to plates of smoked salmon, one of Hamish's catches, and heated nibbles from Marks & Spencer. And, as usual, we turned up looking like the poor relatives, in tattered clothes that my frequent stitching failed to hold together. I don't know why but, unless we dressed in our smart clothes, put away for meetings and weddings, we always managed to look a bit rumpled. It seemed impossible to live in the country and keep clothes clean and pressed. But Hamish and Pam managed. They could have been dragged backwards through the mud and gorse bushes and they would still look immaculate. And the wonderful thing about them was that they apologised to us for looking untidy.

'Oh, that was just Jonathan putting cowls on the chimneys,' I said casually, sipping white wine that had been chilled in the stream.

Hamish was impressed. So was I, I had to admit. After the incident with Willie when he had cleaned our chimneys, we decided that we should do these things ourselves. Or, at least, Jonathan should. And, with the agility of a leopard, he had just nipped up the ladder and leapt across the roof.

Now that the track was clear, John Stuart, astride his quad, herded the sheep back on to the land around us and came by most days to check them. Sometimes he waved, sometimes he didn't. And his son rode close by our windows with his gun and ferret, staring in but looking away if he caught sight of us. They seemed amazed that we were still here. That we had actually made it through our first winter. We sensed a degree of hostility or suspicion. Perhaps we were wrong. Paranoid even. It's easy to read into things in an isolated glen. But then they came by with the tractor and trailer and dumped a whole load of shit in front of the cottage. A winter's collection of dung from the cow sheds. The smell hung in the air and the flies, of the bluebottle and yellow dung variety, collected *en masse*. Perhaps we were right. Perhaps our presence was not welcome.

After its long winter sleep, the highlands seemed to be waking up for the summer. The first wave of tourists hit the scene and jobs for the season began. We, too, were affected by this awakening and picked up enough free-lance photographic work to make us think we might make a living from it. So, with the aid of a regional grant, we had a logo and brochure designed and set ourselves up as the Glenlivet Centre of Photography, which sounded like a much grander outfit than it actually was but, looking to the future, we saw it as an umbrella to encompass a number of growing freelance projects as well as the photography workshops. Pumped up with ideas and enthusiasm, we felt really good about the way things were turning out.

Feeling so good, we had to celebrate. And why not with a cask of whisky. At the Scotch Malt Whisky Society, a colleague had told Jonathan that, with a consortium, he had bought a cask from Glenfarclas. Great. It sounded an affordable way of legally bottling your own supply of cask strength malt whisky and we could easily form a consortium from the family at large, all of whom were, or had been, members of the Scotch Malt Whisky Society. There was my father whose great-grandfather had been the managing director of Bulloch Lade which owned Caol Ila distillery, my brother who is a hard-working doctor and enjoys unwinding with a few drams, his wealthy father-in-law, and Jonathan's father who had also introduced a few Istanbul friends to cask strength malt whisky. So we drove around to the other side of Ben Rinnes to make inquiries at the Glenfarclas distillery. Run by a father and son, we had hoped to meet one of them but there was no way the Englishman in the visitors' centre was going let us past him.

'Why are you interested in a cask?' he asked. 'I don't think you'd be able to afford one,' he added bluntly, looking us up and down with undisguised disapproval.

Dressed in our hill gear – walking boots and fleeces – we may not have signalled wealth but we didn't look like tramps either. Sporty rather than scruffy. More importantly, we were consumed with desire for the pungent, oily nectar that is cask strength whisky. At the Scotch Malt Whisky Society and Cadenheads, we had sampled a vast range of bottlings from most of the distilleries in Scotland and Orkney. Some of which are worth their weight in gold. Conjuring up the smell and taste of sea, wind, heather, hills, spices, scents, and in the words of one description from the Scotch Malt Whisky Society: 'the top of the dung heap'. These are things that Scots have lived for. Some have even died for them too. And we would jump over the moon for a cask strength Ardbeg, Ledaig, Springbank, or Old Pulteney. But we had settled on a cask from Glenfarclas because it was local. And we knew it could be done.

'You should buy this bottle,' the Englishman said,

steering me towards the standard Glenfarclas malt. 'Although the ladies prefer the lighter Tamnavulin.'

I ignored him. I was only interested in cask strength malt whisky. Some of it was exquisite stuff. If you allowed it to be, it was a whole experience. There was the nosing and the delicate beading around the glass, there was the sharp flavour on the front of the tongue and the depth of flavour on the back, before the full flavour filled the mouth. And there was the delicious oiliness. With all that in my mind, why would I be interested in a very ordinary malt?

Meanwhile, in spite of the Englishman's persistent interruptions of rehearsed patter, Jonathan engaged the second-in-command, a local man with ruddy cheeks, in a more casual chat about whisky. Eventually, though, the Englishman butted in with indisputable finality.

'As I said,' he boomed. 'Glenfarclas doesn't sell casks.'

We got back home, no richer in whisky but no money spent, to find a high mound of grey powder dumped outside the gate of Corrunich. Lime to be spread on the ploughed fields. With all the space around us, surely the delivery truck could have taken a wider berth? The wind would blow the dust across our garden and into our windows. It felt like we had become the dumping ground for the farmer's dust and shit.

While drinking at Ladderfoot that evening, Pam generously suggested that it might have been an act of habit. He probably didn't think, she said. He had just always dumped it there. And now that Corrunich was inhabited, he hadn't thought to change his ways. It was convenient for the fields. Pam was probably right but we were less generous in thought. First it was the shit, now the lime. Even if it was habit, surely there was no need to dump them both at our door. And, as we knew the farmer's tenancy of the land around us was recent, we assumed that he hadn't had time to develop habits yet. So, rightly or wrongly, we regarded the dumping as another territorial claim thrust in our faces.

Living where we do, near the rivers Spey, Avon and Livet, it seemed such a shame not to fish. Like villagers who live at the foot of mountains but never climb them or people who live in Edinburgh but never attend the Festival. So we bought one cheap trout rod, as we only had enough money for one, and Jonathan went fishing first. In a stretch of the Livet, overgrown with trees and bushes, in which his line seemed to get frequently tangled. It was while he was busy untangling his line that an old farmer who was out walking approached him.

'You shouldn't have to pay to fish this trickle,' he said.

Life was not the same in these parts, he went on, conversationally. He used to fish the rivers and burns for free. Most of the locals did. Some with a frying pan to fling the catch on to the bank and then cook it over a stick fire.

'Sticks from the wood, fish from the river, and a beast from the hill,' he said with the passion of a poet. 'That's a highland man's right.'

*

Hearing that Jonathan had the fishing bug, Hamish invited him to cast a line on his beat on the Findhorn. As the crow flies it was not that far from the Braes but the climate and scenery were dramatically different. We could have been in another country. A fairly long drive through dense pine forest led to a small wooden hut with a veranda, perched above a deep-pooled bend in the river. Steep red-soiled cliffs, topped with lush green vegetation, had been carved out on either side. With a little stretch of the imagination, it could have been a Colorado canyon or a Rocky Mountain gorge.

While Hamish and Jonathan fished, I took Biglie for a walk in the forest. No moose but lots of roe deer and an infestation of black and red ticks. The long grasses and shrubs were crawling with them. They latched on to my jeans and worked their way up my legs as I tried to flick them off. The red ones were easy to spot on Biglie's thick coat but the black ones disappeared into the deep tufts of hair. My father, as a result of one of his less endearing scientific interests, has photographs that he has taken under a microscope of ticks on a midge and of an ordinary ground beetle with a dozen ticks clinging to its back. Horrible creatures. Just thinking about them makes me feel itchy. And I have been told that once a tick has ballooned with blood and falls off its host, it can live off that blood for up to a year. Then it's time to find a new host. So, after an intensive de-ticking episode, Biglie and I joined the others at the river. A tick-free zone.

Jonathan looked happy. He had borrowed Hamish's

waders and salmon rod and was standing in the middle of the river. Being a novice, I knew he was conscious of holding Hamish up and spoiling his day but the experienced fisherman, who had a reputation for plucking fish out of the water with the ease of a heron, looked perfectly content sitting on a rock watching the river. A moment later, Hamish was shouting at Jonathan through a burst of uncontrollable laughter. So caught up in the excitement of the river, Jonathan had obliviously stepped too deep and his waders were filling up with water. Pam swooped to the rescue. In immaculate attire, she had arrived with lunch. Directly from her kitchen hob to the camp-cooker in the hut. A lamb and apricot casserole, served on china plates, with glasses of chilled white wine.

We were dining at the Taste of Speyside, a small restaurant in Dufftown and the only local place we ever ate out in, when an Italian couple came in. It was late and the restaurant was empty, in fact the kitchen was closed, but the owners, one of whom is the chef, agreed to serve them. As we were already locked in banter with the owners, we drew the Italians in and steered them cheerfully towards the whisky and heather honey cheesecake. And, at the end of the meal, we invited them back for a drink. The kind of friendly invitation we so often took up on our travels. A gesture of hospitality that can make a difference to one's trip.

Coming back for a drink meant a forty minute drive through the hills. At night. So it seemed reasonable to suggest they spend the night. We waited, while in an interlude of rapid Italian, Oliviero and Chiara convinced themselves that this would be all right. When they had arrived in Dufftown they had, in true European fashion, sought a good place to eat before a place to stay so their suitcases were still in the car and they had nowhere to go. It was decided.

At the bottom of our track, I jumped out of my father's Land Rover to warn them about the bumps and puddles. Perhaps they would prefer to leave their car and ride with us, I suggested. It's OK, it's just a hired car, Oliviero said. He'd prefer to drive. We dimmed our headlights – we always do so we don't startle the nocturnal wildlife – and took the track very slowly. Painfully slowly. But still the Italians lagged behind. The darkness seemed to reach before us, never ending. They might be having second thoughts, I said to Jonathan. We laughed through our sympathetic smiles.

I jumped out to open the first gate and let Biglie out of the back of the Land Rover. As I held the gate open for them, I caught sight of Chiara's face momentarily lit by the tail-lights of our vehicle. With the passenger window firmly up, she was sitting rigidly looking straight ahead, clutching her handbag on her knee. The panic on her face said it all. It was the middle of the night and they were up a dirt track with two strangers and a big dog with no sign of civilisation ahead. I waved and, in an attempt to reassure them, pointed to our cottage through the darkness. Of course, they couldn't see a damn thing.

Arriving at the cottage didn't alleviate their fear. At

least, not instantly. For until Jonathan had turned the generator on, it too was in total darkness. I led the couple into the kitchen and fumbled around for a candle which leant a golden warmth to the room and enabled them to look around and calm down. Suddenly, the lights and the radio burst into life. Jonathan had worked his magic in the barn. I poured a grateful Oliviero a stiff dram. Chiara, who looked like she needed a dram, didn't drink.

A couple of hours later, we were still up talking and drinking around the fire. Oliviero, who was a doctor in Venice, spoke good English and chatted about his bachelor life. He loved Venice and preferred to live alone. He didn't want to get married and settle down. Chiara, who spoke only Italian, shared her distress with me. She lived with her family in Padua and wanted Oliviero to move there too. She wanted to marry him.

In the morning, they were, at least, united in their surprise. The darkness had lifted to reveal a quiet, scenic glen basking in sunlight. But, for an Italian, the clincher was the breakfast. The best they had had in Scotland. Warm, freshly baked bread, straight from the oven, and a choice of home-made jams – pear, redcurrant, blackcurrant or raspberry. With *real* coffee. They were surprised that we bothered to make our own bread. But then in Italy, they had no need to, as the still-warm loaves bought from the baker's oven are unbeatable. As if they hadn't eaten for a long time, they tucked in with passion and wished they could stay longer.

*

We parked my father's Land Rover at the back entrance to the Estate house. In a shaded spot beside large pink-flowered rhododendron bushes, so that Biglie wouldn't get too hot. It was a blustery July day but the forecast was for a settled, sunny afternoon. Dressed for the hill, in fleeces and mountain boots, we made our way to the back door carrying camera bags and a tripod. We knew our way around as we had already photographed the interior of the house and gardens for a brochure. This time we had been hired for discretion. To shoot the private visit of President Mugabe to the Estate. Mainly on the hill, John Hammond had said, as it was he who, in his role of Estate manager, had given us the work.

There was no one at the back of the house so we wandered around to the front. There didn't seem to be anyone answering the front door either so we set about looking for the ideal spot from which to photograph the arrival of the president. The Estate lawn was carefully manicured, not a blade of grass out of place, and the sheltered garden brought summer to life with splashes of colourful flowers in bloom. Beyond the garden, the flat countryside rolled out in shades of yellow and bright green. We were really only on the other side of the hills from Corrunich but, once again, we could have been in a different country. In our part of the world, we had barely moved out of spring.

A group of official suited men, two white and two black, approached us. Grampian Special Branch and Mugabe's bodyguards they announced, eyeing us suspiciously, and began to lay the rules for pestering paparazzi. 'Don't worry, we're hired for discretion,' we explained. But the suspicions of one of the bodyguards were not so easily allayed. He detested photographers. 'Do you know Zimbabwe?' he challenged in a heated manner. 'No,' I replied with what I hoped was a charming smile. 'But I do know that Harare is "the city that never sleeps".' A row of perfect white teeth zipped across his face, as he grinned from ear to ear. From that moment, Cornelius, the body-guard of the President of Zimbabwe, decided we were all right.

A taxi drew up at the front steps with an early arrival. A smart, polished-looking guest who knocked confidently on the windowpane of the double front doors and then hung around waiting for someone to let him in. The door opened a fraction to reveal a tall, slim woman dressed ele-gantly in tomato red which set off her mahogany skin. The guest introduced himself to her impassive face and, after what seemed an impolite period of time, she offered her hand in greeting before inviting him over the thresh-old and closing the door firmly behind him.

'A rich bugger, that one,' the taxi driver said, conversa-tionally. 'Flew in his own plane from Hamburg to Aberdeen. Gold and diamond mines in Africa.' We smiled. Having seen the list of guests, we were well aware of their wealth and stature. 'Are you here on holiday?' he asked suddenly, having exhausted the details of his rich passen-ger. We laughed at this absurd question. He must have become so jaded with the sight of photo-snapping tourists that he wasn't surprised where they turned up.

The lady in red had spotted us and hovered in the doorway. We climbed the steps towards her as she slipped out, glancing back furtively, as if she didn't want anyone to see her. 'Who are you?' she asked us with her head cocked to the side. The cameras and tripod should have given the game away but, giving her the benefit of the doubt, perhaps she too thought we were on holiday. 'The photographers,' Jonathan said, patting the Nikon around his neck. 'Ah, right,' she whispered, sucking in her breath. 'Well I don't want to see you or your equipment. Hide behind some bushes and jump out, or whatever you photographers do, when the president arrives.' We were speechless. 'Oh, and help yourselves to tea, coffee, drugs,' she added, as an after-thought. 'Just joking,' she quipped, smiling over our heads. 'My brother's a photographer in London so I know what you're all like.' And then she disappeared inside.

Our brief had been to take photographs of a candid nature, rather than official line-ups, so we decided to take things as they came. We joined Cornelius and the other bodyguard who were staring at the lone piper, in full regalia, warming up his instrument. The sound of heavy wheels crunching gravel made everyone turn and look at the driveway. As if someone had put a bomb up his kilt, the piper leapt into the air and darted over to his designated spot under a swaying willow tree where, with all his might, he blew into his pipes. Muttering that the president was early, the bodyguards and Special Branch rushed over to the front steps and Jonathan and I scrabbled across the lawn to line up with the vehicle carrying the president.

More Special Branch and more African bodyguards headed the convoy. Behind came the splendid-looking Zimbabwean Chief of Police. A hefty man in dress uniform with gold brocade and an assortment of medals pinned to his chest. He looked more presidential than the bespectacled president himself who stepped out of the host's Range Rover in a grey suit. The host exchanged a quick word with his wife, the lady in red, and then ushered Mugabe back into the car. The various dignitaries gathered on the steps looked confused as the convoy moved off again slowly. 'Quick let's go,' shouted Cornelius, rushing towards us. He didn't want to be left behind. Nor did we.

We found my father's Land Rover jammed in by a double-decker bus that had been hired to ferry guests from and to the airport. We had no choice but to crash through the rhododendron bushes and charge after the convoy. Cornelius was enjoying himself in the front seat. 'This is like Africa,' he exclaimed with childlike excitement. 'And I'm so happy that she is black,' he said, clinging on to the dashboard. He was referring to the host's wife, the lady in red. 'I didn't know that before and it's *so* good,' he sang with infectious delight. He wasn't the only one affected by such a discovery. Big, black Biglie, who was in the back with me, was so overwhelmingly delighted with the colour of his new passenger that it took all of my strength to hold him back from licking Cornelius' ears.

The old Land Rover shook and rattled as we sped up the hill track desperately trying to catch up with the convoy. 'I could do with this Land Rover in Africa,'

Cornelius said, patting it with approval. 'How much do you want for it?' I could imagine the horror on my father's face as we explained the fate of his car. *Don't worry it's gone to a good home. In Africa!* No sooner had we caught up and begun to sink into a relaxed pace than the convoy came to a halt. On the top of the hill. Everyone stepped out into the wind to admire the agricultural plains below them. Fortunately, one of us was on the ball. Jonathan crouched low and expertly captured the host, Mugabe, and the Zimbabwean Ambassador on the hillside. I, on the other hand, was trying to disentangle myself from an excited Biglie who had just spotted a phalanx of black men and, by the time I had brushed his hairs off my lens, we were off again. Down the hill and back to the house for lunch.

Special Branch and the bodyguards were fed at the back, in the kitchen, while we hung around the front steps awaiting instructions. Every so often the lady in red would pop her head out for a photo request. The welcoming speeches, signing the visitors' book, Mugabe being piped in to lunch. Her earlier command of an 'out-of-sight' role seemingly forgotten. And then lunch began, the content reminiscent of the worst school dinner, and ended with a special treat for Mugabe. A large wobbly jelly – green, yellow, red and black – moulded into the flag of Zimbabwe. His characteristic scowl was wiped off his face as he surveyed the jelly with delight. It was all too much for the elderly waitress who carelessly dribbled the melting ice-cream, served directly from its cardboard box, down the hostess's red suit.

The warm sunshine predicted for the afternoon drew the guests out on to the front steps for coffee. We snapped guests mingling and chatting and the host hurriedly arranged a few line-ups. The Zimbabwe contingent had to leave for London, bound for Africa. The Chief of Police, who had mysteriously acquired a collection of plastic shopping bags, departed with a secret invitation to me to stay with him in Zimbabwe. Cornelius grabbed us and said a fond but slightly sulky farewell. He was leaving without the Land Rover. And the hostess, much to the astonishment of the gathered guests, said a hasty goodbye and skipped down the steps, swinging a Harvey Nichols bag, to join her husband and Mugabe in the Range Rover.

As the convoy swept out of the drive, a momentary hush settled on the remaining guests. The hostess's departure had come as a complete surprise. They had been left to sort themselves out. With a little help from the host's young and flustered personal assistant who had just learnt that the double-decker bus, hired to transport these very people back to Aberdeen, had already departed. Apparently, Mugabe's bodyguards had got on board and ordered the driver to follow the president.

For those who had time, another bus was called out from Aberdeen. But some of the guests had no time. They had planes to catch. Half-heartedly, we offered to help. With our dog and camera equipment we could only comfortably squeeze in two, at a push three, people. But, for us, it would end up being a four-hour round trip so we were relieved when the Estate keeper picked up the phone and called his son at their home in the middle of the woods. Busy skinning a rabbit, his son said he would have to change his clothes first. 'It's nae matter fit you're wearing,' we heard the keeper tell him. 'Just come.' So he did, spattered in blood. In an ordinary car with room for four passengers. As it turned out that meant three urgent guests and the keeper himself. It was his duty, he said, to drive the host's Range Rover back from the airport. The rest had to wait for the bus.

As our second short highland summer raced by, so did the shooting parties and keepers. The night-time shooting kept up a pace too. Sometimes it was John Stuart shooting rabbits and hares in the fields he had sown, after he had spread the shit and scattered the lime. But most of the time it was the keepers with lights blaring and guns fired from moving vehicles. Being a keeper seems to fit every boy's fantasy – a set of Estate tweeds, an overland vehicle, a gun, and the freedom to roam day or night churning up the ground, popping off everything that moves. A slight exaggeration perhaps as some keepers, like our friend Sandy, are diligent and considerate, but there are others who behave as if they own the land and have no regard for the wildlife or the environment. And no regard for the people living in the open country.

It was a breezy, enchanting evening and I was on my way back from the dams with Biglie when a big, white campervan appeared on the horizon. By the time I reached

Corrunich, it was negotiating the big puddle before the Estate gate and Jonathan was hiding behind a tree looking through his binoculars. What on earth is a camper-van doing on this track? we asked ourselves, as we watched it drive slowly past us towards the next gate. As if struck by our thoughts, the driver stopped the van and reversed into the juniper bushes to turn around. And got stuck. Backwards and forwards he rocked, churning up the ground, until the spinning rear wheel got a grip and sent small stones flying into the air.

'Looking for nature,' the driver drawled in a Germanic-sounding accent as he swanked towards us in that confident, effeminate way of fashionable European men. He was wearing a designer shirt, thin cotton pedal-pushers and natty, leather shoes. We stared at him, trying our hardest to look intimidating. If he had chosen any other track to drive down, he would have been met by much less accommodating glares.

'Zis is lovely nature,' he said, gesturing to the hills. 'Ve vill camp here.' Oh no you won't, I wanted to say. You should go to one of the Estate's designated picnic and camping spots. Why not the one by the old manganese mine which used to be headed with a sign 'beware of the adders' until it was turned over to tourists. But I didn't. I was polite. He was a foreigner. 'Here,' he stressed again, pointing to the ground at his feet. By our gate. I shook my head. Over by the woods, I said, pointing to the ones furthest away. Okay, he agreed, somewhat reluctantly, crumpling his lips and nose so that they touched one another.

'Bloody Belgian,' I muttered under my breath, when I saw the plate of his retreating van. He didn't go very far. In the vast expanse of nature around us, he chose the nearest woods, in the lee of Corrunich. Evidently, his craving for nature meant communing with us.

Hamish invited Jonathan to accompany him stalking. An early start and a long day, over on the Glen Muick Estate. We both got up at dawn and, while Jonathan was getting ready for the hill, I made him a sandwich that would fit snugly into his pocket. A 'piece', or so I had understood. As stalking involves walking and crawling great distances in silence, it is important not to be burdened by extra weight. A 'piece' and handfuls of water from the burns is all you need.

An interesting, but uneventful, morning culminated in a hilltop lunch and the back-up Land Rover drove up to join them. The keepers yanked open the rear door, pulled out their knapsacks and huddled by the vehicle to eat. As Hamish reached in the back, he turned to Jonathan and asked him if he had brought something to eat. Jonathan nodded, indicating confidently to his pocket, and sat down on the ground. Holding a large wicker picnic hamper, Hamish settled down beside him. Neatly and lovingly packed inside was lunch for a hungry stalker – sandwiches, fruit cake, chocolate biscuits, a banana, a thermos of coffee, a small container of milk and one of sugar, and a bottle of whisky with a glass.

Sitting beside his well-prepared companion, Jonathan

munched quietly on his meagre, squashed sandwich thinking of all the delicious things he could have packed if he had known that lunch was going to be delivered by vehicle. He shouldn't have listened to me. But I was the Scot. I should know about these things. And I thought I did. I had grown up with stories of hardy, kilted highlanders who, with their goolies swinging loose, strode off into the hills for the day with only a 'porridge piece', a square of solid, cold porridge that had been set in a drawer, tucked into their sporrans.

The rain fell in torrents. It was almost tropical in its velocity and accompanied by angry thunder. A rare sound in this part of the world. It was late afternoon and I had just stepped into our bedroom when the sky filled with a fiery red glow and a pink streak flashed across the room. Lightning. It struck the branch of a tree, a poor, withered looking larch, already deformed from a previous strike. At that very moment, Jonathan was walking by the tree, on his way to the generator with a newly-filled bucket of diesel. But, mercifully, the lightning just missed him. He really didn't need anything else to go wrong. Not that day. It could be said that his mood was already like that of the sky. Thunderous. Ready to explode. He was in full battle with a new second-hand generator and had been so for days, ever since the first one had shaken itself to death.

At the start of the mushroom season, Monica von Habsburg, a family friend, introduced us to wild mushroom hunting. It wasn't that we needed a Habsburg, nor indeed a Countess for that matter, it's just that her bedroom window looks on to a wooded hillside and, with theatrical persuasion, she is convinced that she can see them popping out of the ground. She even sees them in her sleep. So when she invited us over for lunch, she prepared the fruits of her morning's hunt. Whole *porcini*, sautéed in olive oil and garlic, with sprigs of fresh rosemary and lemon thyme, picked from her garden. We ate them from the pan, outside in the warm sunshine, soaking up the oily pan juices with home-made bread. They were so deliciously tender, they could only be described as the seafood of the earth. And after lunch she led us to her hunting grounds where we collected enough to feed an army.

Back at Corrunich we continued to taste Monica's *porcini* in our mouths. As if seized by an addiction, we kept thinking about them. Jonathan would sniff the morning air to determine if it was a good day for wild mushrooms, particularly *porcini*, the king of all mushrooms. He would enter the woods singing '*porcini*' to the tune of Volare as he hunted for the little plump Bhuddas sitting in the grass. On the day he came back from the woods with his basket piled high with *porcini*, there was a team of workmen on the old lady's roof. As it had been leaking like a sieve, we had got a grant to repair and replace the slates. 'Is that them magic mushrooms?' one of them shouted down, incredulously. He must have had visions of us bombed out of our minds. 'No, they're for eating,' beamed one very happy hunter. Supper was on his mind. 'You wouldn't catch me dead eating them things,' the workman shouted, shaking his head and screwing up his face in distaste. 'I'd rather eat my grandmother.'

John Stuart, the tenant farmer, came in for a dram. A coffee too. Cask strength and freshly ground, respectively. He appreciated both. A man of few words, those that he spoke were slow and deliberate. His eyes, which at one time seemed steely and suspicious, were now warm and smiling, crinkling with a sense of humour. His visit was long overdue. We had asked him in several times but, until now, he had refused. So, in our minds, we had gradually been building a picture of a man who bore us a grudge. Perhaps we had expected too much. It was only natural he should treat us with caution. We were the strangers, the ones who had moved in. And he had seen strangers come and go in the Braes. Just because I'm Scottish, why should I be accepted? Continuity is a myth in Scotland. Accents and actions single you out. And, in the eyes of the local farmers, we didn't look as if we did anything. We were an enigma. Norman was the only one who seemed interested in getting to know us or, at least, he was the only one who asked us questions. Albeit, impertinent ones, at times. But he never gave away much of himself. Highlanders don't. They are intensely private people. So we decided that all this time John Stuart's cool demeanour had been a display of highland reticence. Not a personal vendetta. He had been taking his time to accept our presence. And time is what it takes. Like earning trust in a relationship. Pam was right, he probably hadn't thought about us when he shot rabbits and dumped the shit and lime in front of our home. It had all been in a day's work. Once we began to look at it that way, we completely changed our minds about him and got along fine.

Slowly we were learning to shed our city skins and accept the casual pattern of life in the highlands. No one seemed to be in a hurry. A lot happened, yet nothing really happened. It was like the sleepy Mediterranean in a colder climate. Farmers drove their ancient, wounded vehicles in the middle of the roads at such a slow speed we wondered if they were drunk. Sheep and cows were herded along the minor roads at a leisurely pace. Nobody really went anywhere and they always had time to chat. It was as if we had become caught up in a time warp where patience was a state of being.

But we were in an awkward position. While everyone around us moved at a slow pace, we were desperately trying to catch up with a faster one. From our peaceful, laid-back outpost we had to make a living. We had to extend our net of freelance work beyond the local boundaries. The round of weddings, portraits and Estate events wasn't bottomless. In fact, it had a very definite bottom. One that spanned the summer season. So we had to convince brash, impatient city businesses in the south that we were versatile. That living in the highlands shouldn't be seen as a hindrance. That although we didn't have a phone or fax, we could keep in touch. Few people were convinced and nearly everyone was in a meeting or out to lunch. But we were persistent and spent many hours pushing pound coins into the slot of the cramped phone box, permeated with the stench of urine from the flocks of sheep and lambs that surrounded it. Sometimes we trekked back and forth to the phone box all day. The distance we already felt from businesses in Edinburgh and London was only magnified by our sheer determination. As far as most people were concerned, our very location was north of civilisation. About six hundred miles north to be exact. This deemed us unreliable. And so most of the work continued to come from one source, only. Our friend John Hammond, who passed things our way.

One thing that wasn't slow was the speed with which some publishers rejected our book on Turkish food. Others didn't even bother to reply. Instead, we had to call them. We had sent the proposal to about thirty publishers and, by the end of the summer, we had a clear idea of where our book was going. Nowhere. Yet again, publishers didn't feel Turkey merited a book of its own. But we did. So by using our home as security once more, we dipped further into debt and flew out to Istanbul to soak up the tastes and take fresh photographs.

Staying at the *yalı*, we strolled around familiar neighbourhoods with tall, rickety, wooden houses that flanked narrow, leafy, pot-holed streets, chatting to families sitting in shabby courtyards, doorways, balconies, anywhere they could set up a makeshift table to balance a few dishes. The musical tones of cutlery clattering against crockery, the hot smoky aromas of fish and meat cooking on the outdoor *mangal*, luring us down alleys to a table under the shade of a giant old tree by a village mosque. Shamelessly, we were led by our irrepressible greed to be faced with the mouth-watering dilemma of what to eat – crushed green olives with coriander seeds, small green peppers stuffed with aromatic rice, pine nuts and currants, fish balls flavoured with cinnamon and dill, fried aubergine and courgette served with cooling, garlicky yoghurt, a spicy walnut, cheese and carrot puree, and crisp cigar-shaped pastries filled with finely minced meat. Time stood still while we ate. And ate. Filling ourselves with inspiration. Ready to return to the land of cold porridge and clootie dumpling. To our windswept home in the hills with a rucksack full of spices and ideas. There we would revamp the book proposal and send it out to publishers one more time. As a new book.

'Who is Josceline Dimbleby?' the Iranian publisher asked, looking at our latest proposal. 'And do we have to have her?'

Sitting in his London office, we were amazed he had to ask. We had thought the Dimbleby name would trip off the edge of the tongue in media and publishing circles. As she was a close friend of one of Jonathan's uncles in Istanbul and passionate about Turkish food, we had asked her if she would write the foreword. Very kindly, she had agreed, aware that her name might open doors for us. And it had. Three doors, to be precise. Two of which were closing as we, the author and photographer, were not known – an argument that stands on its head because if you're not given a break on the strength of your work, how do you get known? The third, a publisher of Middle Eastern texts and one cookery book was willing to take that risk. Not the best option, but the only one. With, arguably, the lowest advance in the history of food publishing. And no fee for Josceline Dimbleby, whose very involvement we were having to explain to a London publisher with offices in the heart of the City.

'Her name is of vital importance,' we stressed, without a shred of doubt. 'Not only will it help sell copies of the book, it will also alert the people in the food world to its existence.'

'Point taken,' smiled the Iranian. He was quite charming really. Like a wolf in a sheep's disguise.

At this point, some would say we should have bolted. A track record of one cookery book and no idea who Josceline Dimbleby was should have been indication enough. And the publisher had put the onus on us to find and hire a professional studio, an art director, a food stylist and home economist – the minimum required team for food publishing these days. Surely, we should have held out for a better deal. But, since its conception, it had taken five years to get this book accepted and our tenacity was wearing thin. Anyway, we had no intention of hiring anyone. How could we with that advance, in our remote location? I think the publisher knew that but he was

Middle Eastern to the core. Prepared to take the risk as we were cheap.

No, we had other problems. Ones that only we knew about. The book was to be completed in three months. That would be the end of April. To be published in September of that year. So we would be cooking and shooting the food in our winter. With no fridge. No electricity. No phone. No vehicular access to the cottage. No help and no money. And, according to a professional guide on food photography, we should have had 'a well-equipped kitchen, preferably with gas and electric hobs, two or three ovens, and at least one microwave . . . a good, large freezer and a large refrigerator.' But even these were minor concerns. Our biggest problem was our own audacity. The two of us were about to take on the roles of four or five people, using our primitive kitchen as a studio, in the full knowledge that neither of us had ever professionally styled and photographed food before. And we had only a 35mm camera and an amateur flash to do it with. So, perhaps, it was fitting that we were cheap.

We got back from London to find our track well and truly blocked with snow. Deep and set for the winter. But we were a little better prepared than before as my father had used a pair of old skis to make us a large, sturdy sleigh which made the portage of supplies and gas cylinders so much easier. So while the blizzards blew with their all too familiar ferocity, I cooked dish after dish on our tiny camp-cooker at one end of the cramped kitchen while

Jonathan set up a temporary studio in the window at the other end. And while I kept cooking, he kept shooting, and we couldn't for the life of us get it right. And then we had to eat the food. Mounds of it. For unlike the professionals, we couldn't afford to throw it away.

Before long, we reached a stage where we began to have serious doubts about whether we could pull it off or not. We still couldn't get the lighting right and we ended up with more food than we could possibly eat. So we piled it on to the sleigh and took it down to the bottom of the track, transferred it to the car and drove over to John and Karon, who were happy to oblige as food dispensers. As they had a phone and a fax, they had also elected to act as our office contacts. An office that, with the walk up and down the track, required a four-hour round trip. But, the fact that it existed at all, satisfied the publisher who was completely unaware of the hassle and distance involved. When we arrived, Karon waved a recent fax in the air. The publisher was requesting our presence at a meeting with the newly-appointed project editor, someone with experience in book and magazine publishing. We were to go to London with a selection of photographs.

Back in London we felt like a couple of country bumpkins, dragging our only set of smart clothes in a battered suitcase through the Underground to the tiny flat of our friend Liz in Notting Hill Gate. Since first viewing Corrunich with us, Liz had been up to stay several times and, on the last occasion, she had brought along Ali, who was soon to become her husband. So there was a lot of catching up to do with them and a few other friends, most of whom had successful jobs in London and earned ten times more than we ever did. Finally, when we pulled down the couch, our bed for the night, we couldn't resist a little late-night viewing. It had been over two years since we had turned on a television and that last time had been for the tearful tribute to Freddie Mercury. But, as the box flashed through its midnight menu, which seemed to flaunt narcissistic trash and sex with a cast of famous people we had never even heard of, we felt a pang of longing for our simple life in the distant, snow-bound outpost which suddenly seemed a world away.

We woke up tired and grumpy. Not in the right frame of mind for the meeting which was an hour's journey through heavy traffic. We got dressed and preened in such a hurry that we had no time to get in a flap over the state of my pink snakeskin shoes, which I had grabbed out of the cupboard at home, only to discover now that the toes and heels had been nibbled by mice. I had also forgotten to pack a belt for Jonathan's suit trousers which, since he had lost quite a lot of weight hauling supplies up and down our track, had become disastrously loose. Back into the suitcase went our cowboy boots and other items of bulky clothing that we had travelled down in but, even with the full weight of my bum on top of them, they wouldn't squash in enough for the zip to close properly. So, with Jonathan holding up his trousers with one hand and a bursting suitcase in the other, I picked up the heavy briefcase full of slides and sample cookery books and leapt out into the street to hail a taxi. We had to take the suitcase with us as, straight after our meeting, we were returning home by train. Alas, no taxi stopped and the suitcase burst open spilling the contents on to the pavement. Cursing the shoddy zip, we stuffed our clothes and wash-things back into the suitcase which I had to carry in my arms like a large, bulging sandwich while Jonathan desperately held on to his trousers and the briefcase as we hoofed it to the Underground. When we arrived hot and rumpled at the office in the City to find no one was ready for us, we wondered why we bothered.

Finally, leaving our shabby suitcase downstairs in disgrace, we were ushered up to the top floor to meet the freelance project editor and an in-house project co-ordinator. Miraculously, in the week prior to the meeting, we had finally got to grips with the lighting of the food shots – there was nothing like the threat of an experienced food editor on board to focus the mind – so we had shot several reels of film, styling the food in Anatolian and Ottoman serving dishes with ceramic tiles, bright kilims and colourful silk cloths that we had at home. Apart from the use of a silver sweet fork which was apparently very '1980s', the editor seemed to like them. Our art director should pay attention to the trends, she warned. And we would need to balance the food with some stylised location shots in Turkey. Where, the publisher interjected, we would have to find ourselves another studio and art director for any additional food shots. Again, we nodded in agreement, mentally calculating the increasing debt we would incur. The paid portion of our advance was already spent. At least three times over. But we were impressed with the editor and felt confident that she would steer us in the right direction.

Back in the snow, after the long train ride home, I put on my woolly hat and gloves to grill kebabs outside the back door. We had stacked some bricks to form an enclosure for the sticks and charcoal and placed a steel rack normally used for wiping muddy boots, over the top. When the wind was around the other side of the cottage, the grill worked quite well, tempting Biglie who hungrily hung around the smell of cooking meat. Meanwhile Jonathan was warm in the kitchen setting up the next shot on the table in the window. We would already have selected which cloths, spoons and dishes we would be using but he had to arrange a dummy dish to catch the variable light coming through the window. Having abandoned the amateur flash as it gave the food an unnatural sheen, window light was all we had. Jonathan also had to remove stray Biglie hairs which crept into the shots every time I opened the back door causing a draught to raise them off the floor and float them in the air. No amount of vacuuming seemed to eradicate them. And, as we were in the country, there was the occasional insect on the move, crawling like a black sesame or cardamom seed across the frame. When the shot was finally set up, I would quickly hand Jonathan the food and pick up the mirror, which usually hung in the bathroom, to reflect light into the frame.

Progress was slow. Some days the storms were too fierce to cook outside or too grey to reflect any light. Some days the ingredients froze in our makeshift fridge, the blue bucket set in the snow. And some days the generator broke down and Jonathan would disappear for hours, even days, to fix it. So when a day started out bright I would try to catch up by preparing as many as ten dishes and then, as if some conspiracy was afoot, the light would disappear. Just like that. Gone for days. But the food wouldn't keep and we ate until we were stuffed. At one point we had aubergines practically coming out of our ears – stuffed, grilled, baked, fried and served with yoghurt, stewed with tomatoes, tossed in rice, layered in *musakka*, and boiled into jam. We were so full of aubergine, we feared we might turn into one. If Hamish and Pam walked by *en route* to Ladderfoot, we would stop them and insist they eat and we packaged up *köfte* and stuffed aubergines for Norman and Jean. Game to try anything, he was quite keen but most of the food was too strong for Jean. 'It gives her the shits,' chuckled Norman, whose own constitution was permanently pickled.

And then there was the stuffed mackerel that hung around for days. It was inedible by the time we photographed it. It started out fresh and shiny, straight from the sea, lying on a board as I bashed it gently with a mallet to smash the backbone and massaged it with my hands. This was no sadistic move on my part, just a way of softening and loosening the flesh from the skin so that I could squeeze it from the tail end, like a tube of toothpaste, to force all the flesh out of an opening I had cut just below the head. With the bones removed, the flesh was then cooked with onions, nuts, dried fruits and spices before being stuffed back into the skin to resume its shape once more. At this point the whole fish should have been lightly grilled, cut into slices and served with wedges of lemon – a lavish creation of the Ottoman palace kitchens – but our carefully stuffed mackerel lost all its dignity as it lay in an old bath in the garden to wait out the storms. Until a day of whirling, fluffy, white clouds and bursts of yellow sunshine, when I dashed around to the front of the cottage with the bathroom mirror, dancing in the wind to keep warm, ready to reflect the slightest ray of sunshine back through the kitchen window on to the miserable looking mackerel, which could no longer be photographed whole as parts of it had turned green. Even Biglie, formerly a diner of sheep shit, refused to eat it.

A dozen bulls' testes met with a similar fate. My mother had managed to obtain the testes from her butcher who, much to her embarrassment, loudly announced their arrival when his shop was full of customers. She had asked for a couple but he had obtained a tray full of the large, wobbly mounds which had to be kept in her deep-freeze until we came over to fetch them. A lady who is most comfortable in Country Casuals and entertains religiously from Elizabeth David and Claire Macdonald, she was delighted to get rid of these unmentionable 'things' that lurked in her deep-freeze, taking up valuable dinner-party room. But, on the journey home, they began to thaw out. Rather quickly. As we had no idea of the durability of a severed, raw testicle, we were keen to cook and photograph them as quickly as possible but, as usual, the weather got in the way and the testes were relinquished to the outdoor bath where the foxes and Biglie couldn't get them. Before sealing them off, we removed two to grill and drizzle with melted butter and chilli pepper, the way the village men do in eastern Anatolia. Some believe it increases their virility. Keen to try them, Norman put in an order but, by the time the sky opened up for a shot, the testes were going off. Sloppy and smelly, we couldn't risk them on Norman but, this time, our virile dog didn't refuse. And we haven't been able to look at a bull the same way since.

It was a beautiful, clear starry night when we saw three figures, two big one small, walk through the snow towards us. We were outside hoping to catch the northern lights which often rose like a white spume, filling the horizon with vertical rays that melted into an arch over the silhouetted hills. It was very cold and still. The sky was almost fairytale blue, littered with twinkling galaxies and a sickle moon. The snow was crisp and crunchy underfoot, alerting us to the sound of heavy boots from some distance. We knew exactly who they were. Knowing that they would have to walk all the way back again, whether we were at home or not, only good friends made the effort to walk all the way out to see us in winter. John, in a jolly mood, strode right over to us, his thirst glands primed for a healthy dram. Close behind, Karon appeared with young James, their eight-year-old son, pink in the cheeks from the air and excitement. It had been an adventure for him. Striding out over the snow at night, past the dark woods and scurrying badgers, into oblivion. And they had all come to deliver a fax, urgently requesting pictures and blurb for the publisher's catalogue. After a few drams and some impromptu food, we waved goodbye to our resourceful friends as they trekked back across the snow with a handwritten reply that Karon would type up and fax when they got home about two hours later, around midnight. The best fax service I've ever come across.

Jonathan was in the barn for some time before he emerged with a grim look on his face. I already knew trouble was afoot. I had heard him curse the air with his rage. 'I'm going to piss in your mouth,' he had roared in Turkish. It sounds so lame in English but, clearly, he was beginning to take it all rather personally. Living with a generator was grinding him down. I needed to hear how bad it was. Were we talking hours, days, weeks? I was in the middle of writing text on the computer and we still had photographs to complete. 'I hate this shit,' he replied, wiping the oil off his spanner with an old pair of my pink knickers – all our underwear ends up as rags. 'It's the one thing I hate about this place.' The oil had frozen and seized up the engine and the alternator had ceased to work. It would have to go to Charlie's, he said. And it wouldn't be a simple job. We didn't even discuss it, we just got on with it and dragged the wretched generator through the snow to the car to transport it to Charlie's, where we left it. Finding ourselves without any source of power, we practically moved in with John and Karon to take advantage of their phone, fax and mains electricity. By day I worked on the text at one end of their large dining-room table while Jonathan selected and labelled slides on his light box at the other end. At night we returned home to sleep.

It was while I was in full swing on the introduction that the unexpected happened. The electricity cut out. I couldn't believe it and felt like banging my head on the table. I had just got so carried away with the reliability of mains power that I had cockily plunged ahead without saving any text. John pussyfooted in expecting me to roar like a lioness protecting her cubs. The power should be back on soon, he reassured me, keeping close to the door in case he had to escape my wrath. A JCB in the town had cut a line by mistake, he explained, but it was being attended to. That was some consolation but it didn't solve the fact that I had lost huge chunks of text. Karon brought in a placatory glass of wine and a bowl of herissa dip that she had just made while John remarked on how calm I seemed. And I was calm. But only because I was desperately trying to memorise the text. Word for word.

All of a sudden we were on a plane to Istanbul, leaving problems of power behind. Throughout our trip in

Turkey, we would not only have mains electricity, although its reliability there can be equally unpredictable, but we could also be contacted by fax and phone. An irony which didn't escape the publisher who, with a touch of humour, remarked that we would be leaving the Scottish highlands to bask in Eastern civilisation. This was to be the final leg of our book. An opportunity to rustle up some Turkish interest in the book, a chance to double-check details and, of course, the required location photographs. But, as our luck would have it, it rained and rained and rained. The skies were washed a slate grey and all the market stalls were covered in sheets of grubby plastic. Heads were hidden under umbrellas or topped with makeshift hats fashioned out of plastic bags. And the street sellers with their baskets and trolleys of food were splattered in muddy water by passing cars. Plenty of material to document on black-and-white film but little that would sit well in a cookery book. It is, undeniably, the reality but people don't want to see fish floating in buckets of dirty water drawn from the polluted Golden Horn or tomatoes being wiped clean with a bit of spit and an oily cloth. So, with the delivery deadline looming and the timing of our trip too early for colourful shots of harvests and blossom, Jonathan set about excluding the debris to isolate a few palatable images.

Back home, we held a goodwill ceremony for our book to wish it well on its journey. It just seemed the right thing to do. So we burned incense and danced spontaneously to the beat of a drum and then we parted company with the completed work, *Classic Turkish Cookery*. Like a baby, it had absorbed every wakeful hour of the last three months and we suddenly felt lost without it. And then, apart from a fax to say that the project editor was no longer on board, we didn't hear anything for months. We knew her departure would mean a delay but that wasn't unusual for publishers and, anyway, the proposed September publication of the book had always seemed unlikely to us. So we left our hard work to its fate and headed off to the west coast for a break in the Knoydart wilderness, armed with a bottle of champagne for Jonathan's birthday, blissfully unaware of how long the delay would be.

After an eight mile trek along Loch Hourn, we camped at the foot of Ladhar Bheinn. The mist came in with the midges, filling the air with the density of a snow-storm. The smoke from the stick fire couldn't clear them away. We got mild relief from Jungle Juice, hoods and gloves but poor Biglie was pestered relentlessly as they attacked his nose, lips, eyes and balls until they were all swollen into deformity. Even the shelter of our two-man tunnel tent and sleeping bags gave us little respite as the midges rode in on Biglie who slept on our feet. There were a few other tents in the designated camping spot but, once all walkers were on the hill, they were swallowed up by the space and we didn't see another soul until we returned to the car park at Kinloch Hourn where the local man in charge of parking welcomed our bag of rubbish. The Dutch and Scandanavians were really good at lifting their rubbish, he informed us, but the Brits just left it behind. Certainly the litter had surprised us, just as it does in the hills around our home. Empty cigarette packs, sweet wrappers, crisp bags, even bottles. The dumping of laziness and a complete lack of regard for nature. But, aside from the litter, our little break had put us in a positive frame of mind and we returned home ready to take on a new dog, a much-needed pal for Biglie, and a dreaded visit to the bank.

Funnily enough, the meeting with the bank manager went more smoothly than the introduction of a new pup into Biglie's comfortable life. Once again we had to borrow money, using our home as security. We knew we were taking a big risk but it was the only way to move forward with other projects and, on the strength of our forthcoming book, the bank manager was very obliging. Biglie, on the other hand, took one look at the fluffy, white thing and growled, sending the bewildered pup into a corner where, with his back to the room, he howled and howled. He was so white with black eyes, he looked like a polar bear cub but, as we wanted to give our new puppy a Turkish name, we called him Aslan, which means lion, as the word for bear sounds like a cry of pain when shouted into the wind. We hoped that his cowardly nature and puppy smell would win Biglie over as there was no question about who would be the dominant dog. For the first few weeks Biglie just ignored the little nuisance that had come to inhabit his home, occasionally snapping at him when the pup came to investigate his food, so we made sure that one of us tired out Biglie on long walks while the other played with the pup to give them both the reassurance and space they needed. It was just a matter of time before Biglie and Aslan became friends, the big black dog tolerating his ears being chewed, his face being sat upon, and his blanket being tugged out from underneath him as he tried to sleep. And so it goes on. Biglie bullies Aslan and Aslan pesters Biglie but most of the time they get on famously.

At the end of September we joined the twentieth century and put in a phone line. We were in two minds about it as we savoured the distance and peace that not having a phone gave us. But there was no escaping the fact that it was crucial for work. As each year swept by us, we had looked into it but BT had hit us with a quote of five thousand pounds every time. Like the quote from the hydro, we couldn't afford it so it took us some time to find a way of doing it ourselves. Legally, of course. Back in June we had found an extremely obliging BT engineer who had helped us get the cable and draw up the plans which, as we live on a Crown Estate, had to be submitted to the Crown factors. We called them with regularity to chivvy them up, citing the hours of lost work they were costing us. The BT engineer called them too. Finally, with no word of apology, the factors admitted they had lost the plans. So the BT engineer drew up another set and this time delivered them to the factors by hand. We were quite glad he hadn't involved us as the last time we had been to the offices of the Crown factors, the head factor led us into a cupboard for our meeting. As neither of us fare well in confined spaces, it was a less than comfortable meeting, hampered further by the view up the factor's hairy nostrils as he stood over us with his back against the closed door while we sat directly in front of him on the only two chairs. Short in stature but not bravado, the factor, with his military-style moustache, seemed to be in his element and quite oblivious to the inappropriate dimensions of his meeting room.

Again the Crown factors took their time to approve the plans. It was such a simple thing that should have taken them minutes, but they were in no hurry. We were though. We were fast approaching the end of September and could get snowed in from mid-October onwards, so we directed our energy to the phone box once more. After a number of calls in which the secretary, in a rather condescending manner, fobbed off our polite inquiries, Jonathan got so fed up that he put on a loud, posh voice, with just the right degree of pomposity and authority to make the secretary buck, and demanded to speak to someone in command as he was rather disappointed with the way in which his situation had been conducted. There was no need to specify the situation or even give his name for, in a matter of seconds, the secretary put him through to one of the factors who swiftly approved the plans the next day.

At last the work could begin. Just as an Indian summer burst through the overcast skies. Jock, the digger-boy, sweltered in the cab of his machine as he dug a deep trench the whole length of the track while Jonathan, dripping with sweat, laboured behind removing all the large rocks and boulders. Together they laid the line and covered the trench and, as a souvenir for all that hard work, we kept one of the large wooden cable spools as a practical table that can be rolled around the garden to catch the sun. A few days later, two friendly BT engineers came out to fix the interior wiring and connect us to the exchange. Joining us for coffee in the kitchen, they began to tell us about some of the other unusual properties they'd been to. 'There was one right posh house where the old woman was so rich she hung her plates on the walls,' one of them recanted. 'You would think plates were for eating off, not for looking at,' he reasoned, shaking his head and chortling at the memory. We laughed and his colleague, seated directly opposite him, smiled politely as he desperately tried to send eye messages across the table at the same time. Hooked on the subject of the old woman and her plates, the chatty one started up again. This time he received a sharp kick to his shin. Wincing in pain, he glared at his attacker. I giggled quietly into my coffee. They would laugh about it later when the chatty one would find out that all the time he had been talking he had been seated with his back to a wall hung with an array of colourful, ceramic plates from Turkey.

The first ring of the phone was like a rude intrusion. Neither of us wanted to answer it. It was the first time a phone had ever rung in Corrunich and the old lady must have shuddered at the vulgar sound. But the first person turned out to be a welcome voice. It was Jonathan's friend, Shan. 'About time, man,' he said. 'I can sleep at night now.' Shan, who lived in the populated ethnic boiling pot of south London, had always maintained that we lived in such a scary place that anything could happen and no one would know. He, too, had seen *The Shining*. You must get a phone, he had insisted time and again. 'You watch too many movies,' had been our standard reply. But the time had come and now, after almost three years of sporadic contact, Shan could call up his old friend whenever he liked. Which is roughly every two or three days.

The second and third calls really were intrusions. Double-glazing and fitted kitchens. Persisting on Sunday afternoons and early evenings. Night and day. Like humming mosquitoes. 'I'm sorry to bother you, Mrs Basan, Boson, Basin, Basoon . . .' Why say you're sorry when you're not? And, most annoyingly, when we actually did want to put in double-glazing, not one of these pestering companies would do it. We were much too remote, they complained. Way out of their area. So why did they bother us in the first place? And, like idiots, still do.

Now that we had a phone, we thought we had better inform our publishers. We could hear their sighs of relief travel all the way up the line from the City to our highland outpost. Some of the staff had apparently been panicking about us being out of contact. They couldn't believe we didn't have a phone. 'Where on earth do they live?' one of them had asked our project co-ordinator. 'The back of beyond?' Well, yes, they do actually, the co-ordinator had replied.

Our third winter started early, the longest and coldest for some twenty years. And I discovered I was pregnant. At the same time, Jonathan's parents came to stay. So, with four adults and two big dogs holed up for weeks on end in a tiny cottage with the constant smell of cooking and cigarette smoke, I reeled with unrelenting nausea. Then, shortly after Jonathan's parents left, I had one of those inexplicable antenatal scares which put me in hospital, two hours away in Aberdeen. We were lucky it turned out to be nothing but, as we trudged back home through the snow, it highlighted how isolated we really were. Our doctor reckoned that, as far as getting pregnant women to hospital is concerned, we lived in one of the most difficult parts of the British Isles. One would think it would be more difficult for those on the islands but, apparently, they are brought into hospital in advance. We would just have to wing it when it happened. At one time, though, the women of this glen must have been really tough. The winters were harsher and women gave birth at home. Some of the locals, like Norman, have never moved from the very spot they were born in. But, all experiences are relative and I was made of softer stuff, relieved that the actual birth was to be in the summer as giving birth in the depth of winter, with no possibility of a vehicle reaching the cottage, would have meant being airlifted. If I was lucky. And, unlike those hardy women of the past, in the event of an emergency, I even had the luxury of a phone.

Back home we holed up in our bedroom with the dogs. It was the only place we could get warm. Under the covers in front of the small fire. Outside, the storms were merciless and unforgiving. The freezing temperatures roamed from minus 25 °C to minus 30 °C. It wasn't much warmer inside. We didn't have double-glazing or carpets at that stage so the freezing gales and fine powder snow blew in through our rickety windows and up through the floor-boards. For weeks we holed up, only venturing out to walk the dogs, fill the generator, and go to the doctor for the antenatal check-ups. And one day, returning from a check-up, we got the car stuck. So while I trudged home through the snow with Biglie, Jonathan spent the next three hours trying to dig the car out but the wheels froze solid and the clutch burnt out in the process. The car was going nowhere. The next day a farmer helped pull the car out with his tractor and Jonathan left it at the bottom of the track where it stayed for days until Charlie was able to come and tow it away. With the freezing temperatures and ensuing bouts of flu, our lives rapidly became unpinned. We ran out of gas for the hot water and the camp-cooker. We ran out of food. We had no car and very little money. But we did have a phone so we rang Hamish and Pam. Could they bring us some supplies if they were planning to come down to Ladderfoot at all? They weren't planning to come, they said, but absolutely insisted on driving all the way out from Forres to drop off relief packages and a gas tube at the end of the track.

As each cold, bleak day went by, I couldn't seem to shake off the flu and slipped into a depressed state of mind. Having been brought up to think positively, it was most uncharacteristic. Attack the day is what I had had drummed into me, both at home and at school. Get up early and get dressed. Don't lounge around. If you start the day with physical discipline, your mind will follow suit. Don't use expressions like 'I couldn't care less' or 'I can't be bothered'. Thump, thump, thump. Until it was drilled in. Now I find that one of the few things that I do find depressing, apart from all the obvious global horrors and disasters which are out of our control, is laziness and negativity in people around me. Optimism feeds the soul but pessimism drains it. So I was thoroughly annoyed to find myself in bed feeling depressed but, with the worry of our increasingly desperate situation weighing heavily on my mind, combined with flu and antenatal nausea, there didn't seem a lot to be positive about. How were we going to cope? I asked myself again and again. Where was the wisdom in bringing a baby into this isolation? We were completely cut off from other people's lives. If we had an emergency, we would have to walk out in freezing conditions. We were up to our eyeballs in debt with little relief on the horizon. And it wasn't from lack of trying. There just was no freelance work in the winter. Everything closed down. We had started working on some new book proposals which we hoped would ride on the back of *Classic*

Turkish Cookery but it had to be published first and we had no idea when that would be as the publishers kept moving the date. We seemed to be in a state of inertia and I loathe sitting idle. I couldn't help feeling that we were being sucked into a hard, lonely lifestyle and we only had ourselves to blame. From where I sat, it was turning into the winter of hell.

But thank God for Billy Connolly. A true optimist. He managed to keep us on the brighter side of down. At the beginning of winter, to keep my mind off the constant nausea, we had hired a video machine so we dug out all our old Billy Connolly tapes and laughed until our sides ached. I then read *Touching the Void*, Joe Simpson's horrifying account of his narrow escape from death in the depths of an icy crevasse. What the hell am I complaining about? I asked myself, angry that I had allowed my thoughts to verge on self-pity. In our own way, we had to find ways of surviving but we didn't even know the meaning of *real* survival. We were just experiencing a severe dosage of the winter blues. A long, hard winter can be grinding. In isolation with aching flu, antenatal nausea, and constant worrying, it was exhausting and depressing. But it will pass. We will be reborn in the spring. The changing of the seasons has always had a profound effect on the psyche.

And then Hyakutake passed overhead. A big white comet with a green tail, like a sting-ray floating in the galaxy. About ten million miles away, but almost within reach. As it crossed our clear northern sky, it stayed with us for days as if it was reluctant to continue its journey. It won't be back for thousands of years. If that couldn't lift our spirits, what would?

The spring and summer of that year passed in a blur. Summer always does. It's a time of easy living, spent outdoors as much as possible. Refreshed by the change of seasons, we busied ourselves with the new book proposals. We had come to the conclusion that, for the time being, we should concentrate on food. The experience of doing *Classic Turkish Cookery* had whet our appetite. We had plenty of material for two new books and we had just bought ourselves a fridge, which would make the food preparations a lot easier. As we still had no constant source of electricity, the fridge ran on gas, which meant we would have to lug an extra gas cylinder through the snow in winter. For the time being though, we were thrilled with our new acquisition. It was the only modern thing in the kitchen and had been surprisingly difficult to find. Plenty of places sold gas fridges for caravans but they were so small, we were just as well off with our bucket. To get anything bigger, we had had to turn to Sweden where they make large gas fridge-freezers for domestic use. And, as it was summer, we immediately filled it with cans of Coca-Cola and ice-cream. The things we hadn't been able to keep sufficiently cool in our bucket for over three years.

There was also no end to the jobs around our home, with repairs and improvements to be made before the arrival of our first baby. For a start, we had to reclaim the bathroom for its original function. All photographic chemicals were banished to the barn, where they remained untouched for some time. And, in between the bits of free-lance work that had picked up again, I tried to keep as fit and healthy as possible for the impending labour. All first mums worry about going into labour and how they will cope, but my biggest worry was if we would get to hospital in time. First there was the slow, bumpy, pot-holed track to navigate, then there was the two hour journey to the hospital. Some of the local farmers joked that they had plenty of rope and years of experience with the 'coos', which was little comfort at that moment as, although I felt large enough to be a 'coo', I didn't fancy having my baby delivered like one. But the scary thing was that there actually could be a slim chance that I would end up in their sheds anyway.

The final proofs for our book arrived on the day our baby was due to be born so I attended to them immediately, aware I could go into labour at any moment and they would lie on the desk for days, weeks even. As it turned out, I entered the gestation period of a much larger mammal, and was booked in to the hospital for induction when the baby was two weeks overdue. I had escaped the farmers' rope and the inevitable embarrassment, not to mention the excruciating indignity. Instead, I had four days of sheer agony and a more acceptable indignity at the hands of caring midwives. Once the induction got under way, I drifted in and out of labour for three days, while a worried Jonathan and two confused dogs came and went the distance. Each day Jonathan arrived with fresh cherries and grapes, so that I didn't have to eat the hospital stodge and, in between the irregular bouts of contractions, he walked the dogs on Aberdeen beach. On the third day, my womb was scraped in the hope that it would speed things up so, in expectation, Jonathan spent an uncomfortable night in the chair beside my bed and the dogs spent a cramped one in the tiny three-door Subaru that we had bought with the appallingly low sum we had received from the insurance of the smashed one.

Early the next morning, Jonathan took the dogs down to the beach again and then I was wheeled into the labour ward to have my waters burst and a needle inserted into my arm to hook me up to an oxytocin drip to increase the contractions. As the drip is known to make the contractions longer and more painful than usual, I was prepared for battle. But, when the contractions came every minute and lasted for one and half minutes with such an intensity they flew off the scale on the graph, I could stand it no longer and gladly accepted pain relief. Neither gas nor morphine took the edge off the pain that gripped my body in such agonising spasms. It felt like a razor-sharp alien was cutting, stretching, kicking and pushing in every way it could to crush my spine and force its way out of my arse. It was like torture. All my years of swimming training, running and hill walking came into use with the breathing, so the baby was quite comfortable, but I was exhausted with the combat. Only an epidural, inserted into my spine, curbed the pain and I was able to rest before the final battle. At that point, Jonathan, who was visibly in a different kind of pain at the sight of my agony, announced that we shouldn't have any more children. He didn't want me to go through that again. And then he went off to feed and walk the dogs and get some much-needed air himself.

Three shifts of midwives later, the final battle took place in the theatre. This baby just did not want to come out. The ventouse, a vacuum extractor, didn't work so our first baby was born, two-and-a-half weeks late, by forceps. Apart from looking like she had been scalped by the failed ventouse and clamped too tightly by the forceps, she was fine. Robust, well nourished, with a good set of lungs and almost tanned looking. I, on the other hand, was bruised, battered and exhausted. I felt like I had been in the cow shed after all. Jonathan, who was both shattered and relieved at the same time, was told to remove his theatre gown and wait for me in the labour room. Where he waited rather a long time, because the third midwife had forgotten all about me. During my labour, she had been dotty and clumsy, a bit like a character in a Carry On film, frequently nipping out for a cup of tea and forgetting to do the things she had said she would do, like bring me a glass of water, and every time she had leant over me to feel my pulse, she had knocked the drip and the needle in my arm. On the way to the theatre, she had got the drip hooked round the handle of the door as she pushed the bed through it and when she had strapped my ankles in the stirrups, she had yanked my hip so wide that I heard something snap. So, once our baby was born, I was not surprised to find myself in the most undignified position imaginable with my ankles still in stirrups, unable to move as I was paralysed from the waist down, left all alone in the theatre. The obstetrician and his team had all gone to wash and change and move on to the next emergency and my midwife had disappeared. God knows what she was doing, but it took her a good half hour to come back for me. I could barely walk for eight months afterwards as my hip had been jerked too far and I had been left in that position for too long, but the hindrance of limping painfully up and down our track was yet to come.

Once I was slotted into the post-natal ward in the early hours of the morning, Jonathan had to make the long journey home. Everyone was asleep in the ward and he wasn't allowed to stay a moment longer. I worried about him driving as he was so exhausted. Before long, though, I had a problem of my own. I was desperate for a pee but, because I was still paralysed from the epidural, I couldn't reach the button on the wall to alert a midwife, so I had to wait in utter discomfort until the six o'clock round. When the gentle, but slight, midwife helped me out of the bed, I collapsed on to the floor as I had no feeling in my legs. Once I was relieved and washed, I was returned to bed but, no sooner had I shut my eyes for the first time in twenty-four hours than the curtains were pulled back and the breakfast trolley clinked its way around the ward. And so began the lack of privacy, the prodding and poking, the questions and the pressure to breast-feed. All in the airless, over-heated ward. It beats me how some mothers actually enjoy their stay in hospital. I couldn't produce milk straightaway, I was too exhausted, so I was clamped into an electric breast pump, which really did make me feel like a milking cow. The ward sister, who seemed to lack any sensitivity, remarked that with large breasts like mine I should be spouting milk, not producing a mere trickle. So, once again, I was clamped in and left. When the sister didn't return in five minutes, as she had said she would, I turned the pump off. Just in time. As I extracted myself from the pump, a thin layer of skin peeled off too. Now I had sore breasts, raw nipples and no milk. I felt the surge of tears welling up in my eyes. I just wanted to go home. To the fresh air and the space. To the familiar hills and whistling wind. But, as our baby, who still didn't have a name, had lost weight, I wasn't allowed to go home until I was able to produce milk. So I fed her as much bottled milk as I could, while my medical parents had a word with the sister and the paediatrician. It was agreed I could go home the next day if our baby gained a little weight. The bottled milk did the trick. So I and my skinned nipples, and our nameless baby, squeezed into the cramped Subaru along with the dogs to make the long, strange journey home. I say strange because suddenly we were on our own with her. This little being that had been inside me for so long was now strapped into her car seat. She was no longer a bump, but a real person, oblivious to the world around her. Her whole future was in our hands. And the realisation that we had no mums, brothers, sisters or neighbours around to help was quite daunting. We would be completely on our own from then on. And I worried about feeding her. I was determined to do it myself but I had no idea when my milk would come in. I needn't have worried, though, as once we got our tiny bundle home to the tranquillity and seclusion, my breasts swelled up like tight water-melons and burst forth. It must have been the fresh air. The next day the doctor made his official visit. It was the first time he had been out to our home and he was quite taken by it. The view, the isolation, the sound of the wind in the trees. 'I don't think I could live here though,' he admitted. 'I'd find myself popping Prozac, talking to spoons.'

When we registered our baby locally, we received a very cool greeting at the door of the registrar's house. Without saying a word, she led us into her sitting-room where her husband was seated on the couch and, while she silently prepared our papers, he launched into a tirade of abuse about the Braes and the people who lived there. It was he who, with religious conviction, told us that when God made the Earth, he made the Braes last. We had thought long and hard about a name for our baby. Finally we had settled on one with Turkish roots that could be pronounced easily in Scotland. But, when we registered Yasmin Shalini Başan (pronounced 'Bashan', not like part of the bathroom plumbing), the registrar eyed us sourly as if we had just confirmed her suspicions that we were the hippies who lived in the hills. I wondered what she would have thought of Jonathan's first choice of name, Alabama.

The arrival of a baby did change the attitude of some of

the locals. Just as my father's old Land Rover had done, the baby raised us a notch or two higher in their estimation. A couple on their own can cause suspicion and rumour. A baby makes sense. It conveys a degree of permanency. A new family in the Braes was certainly rare. Norman and Jean, and John Stuart and his wife, Mary, all arrived bearing gifts while the old lady, bathed in warm August sunlight and filled with flowers from my mother's garden, looked thoroughly delighted with the new life within her walls. It must have been at least fifty years since the last Corrunich baby.

In the autumn we ran out of water. Our spring just dried up. Uncharacteristically for the highlands, we had to pray for rain, shaking our Mexican rain stick at the sky. In the meantime, we had to wash. The streams were so low and mossy we could only collect enough water for basic needs so, once again, we rang up Hamish and Pam at their home in Forres. Would they mind if we bathed at Ladderfoot? Of course, they didn't. And, luckily for us, their water-table was plentiful. So every evening, like a family outing to the *hamam*, the three of us set off with soap, towels and a clean nappy to bathe in the smart, gold-tapped bathroom down the track and then we filled up containers with water for drinking and washing back home.

One afternoon, before heading off for our bath, a plane fell out of the sky. Actually, it was a glider but, at first, we thought it was a plane. Its silent, dark shadow crossed over our rooftop, inches above the chimneys, and dropped into a field beyond the cottage. Just as silently, the pilots stepped out and headed over to us. They needed to phone their club rescue vehicle. While they waited to be rescued, we collected more water from the stream and made them endless cups of coffee, pointing out that the facilities for relieving themselves were outdoors. Anywhere they liked.

Puzzled by our minor drought, Jonathan did a little bit of detective work with a set of home-made diviners. Using two separate pieces of wire, each pushed through a stub of copper tubing which he gripped on to, he walked the route of the underground piping. Until one of the local farmers had shown us this trick, we had admittedly been sceptical, but it really worked. Whenever the diviners detected water, or some underground current, the floppy pieces of wire crossed in a definite manner. In this way, Jonathan discovered there was a second water-pipe leading from the water tank on the hill to our cottage and that the route of that pipe passed right through the middle of a huge wet patch in the grass just below the track. There were only two possible explanations for such a patch: an underground spring or a burst pipe. Just to be sure, Jonathan asked Angus, the local plumber, to come and have a look and he too got out a set of home-made diviners to trace the route of the piping. More accustomed to sceptics than converts, Angus was surprised that Jonathan had used diviners and confided that they were his most reliable tools. He had found water sources where people had thought there were none. As he walked up and down the land, holding the diviners in front of him, Angus was absolutely certain the wet patch was caused by a burst pipe so he began to dig. In a matter of minutes, his suspicions were confirmed. Not only had the pipe burst but it was the pipe that took the water from the tank on the hill to our mains tap. A different pipe to the one we had believed to be carrying our water supply along the route that Alan and Dalla had drawn on the original map. Whether the water-table had dried up solely because of insufficient snow-melt the previous winter or because the water had been spilling out on to the land, we didn't know for sure but, if the water-table had already been low, this leak would have drained it completely. What we did know was that the pipe must have been burst for a long time as the wet patch had been there ever since we had arrived at Corrunich but, as we had had no reason to suspect it had anything to do with our water supply, we had never given it much thought.

Before the onslaught of winter, we sold the second Subaru Justy. Apart from the fact that it was riddled with problems and, due to the hammering it got on the track, it spent more time at Charlie's garage than on the road, it was also no longer practical with three of us and two big dogs. Besides, with a baby to think of, we needed a more reliable, high-set vehicle for our track and the severe winter conditions so we looked at a number of Land Rovers and ended up with a rather smart second-hand one. We were not really in a position to own such a good-looking, comfortable machine and we couldn't help feeling that we must look as if we'd stolen it. Again as we drove around the area, the locals stared and stopped to ask how much it cost. 'If anyone needs one of these, it's you,' acknowledged one of the local farmers. 'It's ridiculous how many people own these things and never take them off tarmac.' We certainly lived in Land Rover terrain so it wasn't long before ours looked well-used, splattered in mud and dust, and we could sit in it without too much of a guilty conscience.

On Hogmanay, Norman and Jean came to first-foot us. After tucking up all the animals for the night, they arrived on foot at midnight. And they didn't leave until dawn. Jean looked pretty, her features softened with a touch of blue eyeshadow and blue-green earrings, both of which lifted the colour of her eyes, but it was Norman who took our breath away. He had spruced up and trimmed his beard. He even had on a clean pair of dungarees and, when he took off his hat, we saw his melon-head for the first time. I don't know what I had expected to be under that hat, a little more hair I guess, but with his head fully revealed, cropped and pruned, he looked younger and softer than the burly bear we were used to. But he was still a rogue. 'D' yae need a hand?' he asked cheekily when I slipped off to breast-feed a hungry baby. 'I'm not one of your heifers,' I replied, which sent him into a spluttering guffaw. 'Is that you sooked dry?' he asked unabashed when I returned to the room.

We felt honoured to see in the New Year with Norman and Jean, our nearest neighbours and the only other inhabitants of such an exposed place. Nobody else knew how wild the winters could be and they weren't nearly as wild as the winters of Norman's youth. They had chosen to walk through the snow to us instead of the annual get-together at the Pole Inn. 'I win all the bets at the Pole,' Jean boasted jovially. 'They always say you two won't make it through another winter, but I know you will.'

The following spring, *Classic Turkish Cookery* was finally published. It had taken the publishers two years but, for us, it had been a long, seven year journey since we had first presented a book of Turkish food to publishers in New York. So it was a huge relief to hold the finished work in our hands. As we had spent the winter setting up publicity for the book, it seemed as if it suddenly took on a life of its own. The calls and reviews kept coming. Behind the scenes we had a little help from Josceline Dimbleby and Fat Lady, Clarissa Dickson Wright, whose presence encouraged the food writers of the main newspapers to review it. Nigel Slater generously gave over his slot on the *Observer* while he was on holiday and Claire Macdonald wrote a glowing review in *The Herald*. Turkish Airlines promoted it in their in-flight magazine and the Turkish Embassy agreed to host the launch in May. First though, completely out of the blue, Scottish Television with, I suspect, a little push from Clarissa, contacted us to be part of their series, Square Meals.

Jonathan and I were exhausted before the STV production team had even arrived. We had been up half the night preparing food for the various sequences and we had got up early that morning to clean the kitchen and get Yazzie, as our baby was now known, fed and dressed and entertained a little before the big strangers took over her home for two days. Our friends, John and Karon, had also arrived early. Karon had come to help look after Yazzie and John was to be in charge of the barbecue, which he had made for us out of a halved oil drum. But, as the foul weather put an end to any plans for outdoor cooking, we resorted to Plan B. Moving the barbecue into the barn. With its cobbled floor, old stable structures and logs piled high, it looked appealing and rustic, not in the least bit Turkish, but that didn't matter as the focus of the programme was to be more on how two people produced such a book in the Scottish highlands. To lend the barn some atmosphere, John and Jonathan cleared it of any junk and then hung up some old pots and pans and a Tilly lamp. They then lit the barbecue to keep warm.

The production team arrived in a barrage of sleet and mud. Some tall, some short, they all huddled in our tiny kitchen for warmth while we had coffee and ran through the sequence. A certain amount had already been discussed and planned over the phone but now they had to work out how and where to shoot each sequence. And there was the question of the generator. They had already deducted the fee normally paid out for the use of electricity, the use of diesel didn't seem to count, and they had brought along their own generator in case ours didn't power their lights. They were all perfectly pleasant but it became apparent very quickly that not one of them had any real interest in food. Square Meals was just another production and the young, chatty presenter was much more interested in talking about snowboarding. As it was our first role on television, we had already accepted that we would make fools of ourselves, but when I saw the chaos around me I felt much more comfortable about the whole thing. I felt even better when the presenter kept fluffing her lines and had to repeat them over and over again. I had thought I would be the only one doing that. She seemed quite natural in front of the camera but, in between takes she was so disinterested in what was going on that she just didn't concentrate. Then when the camera was ready to roll she would turn to me with an earnest expression, the urge to smile twitching at the edges of her mouth. At one point I gave her a piece of flat-leaf parsley to try as she had never seen it before but, as soon as she began to chew on it, she gagged and raced over to the kitchen sink to spit it out. The flat-leaf parsley was too strong for her. Obviously the gagging had to be cut and the sequence repeated and the whole process became rather long and tedious.

By the time it was Jonathan's turn to cook, he and John were almost baked in the heat of the barn. While the camera was on Jonathan, who nervously ran through an entire dish in an uncharacteristic fast-talking London accent, John cooled off with a beer in the rain. As Jonathan reached the climax of his sequence, he discovered to his horror that he'd forgotten one of the principle ingredients so he and the presenter had to start from the beginning again. Meanwhile, I tried to console a distraught Yazzie. It was the first time she had ever been without me and, in spite of Karon's patient efforts, only her mum would do. So I put her in a pack on my back, as I often did when I was cooking, and chatted to her while I made preparations for the next sequence. When the team came back into the kitchen, they thought Yazzie on my back was a nice touch so there she remained while I cooked.

At about six in the evening, in accordance with union regulations, most of the team left to eat in Tomintoul. The producer and her assistant stayed behind and helped to wash dishes and set up the supper scene they intended to film that night. When the others didn't turn up on time, the producer began to get worked up and she and her assistant drifted off to the warm barn for a quiet seat by themselves. It turned out that the delay had been caused by our track. One of their vehicles had got stuck so Jonathan and John took the Land Rover over to pull them out. By the time the whole team and their vehicles were back in our yard, the producer decided that it was too late. The supper scene would have to be postponed to the next morning. Before heading off to Tomintoul for the night, they took a quick shot of the cottage lit up in the dark and then peace descended on us and the exhaustion oozed out of our pores.

John and Karon stayed on for some wine and food, of which there was plenty from the day's filming. As we unwound, we began to dissect the day. We decided that the one thing that we had lacked was professional direction. There had been no one to advise us on how to speak, what to wear, when to look at the camera and how to groom ourselves for the bright lights. We had both looked exhausted, with faces scrubbed clean rather than made up, and we had worn the same clothes all day. The presenter, on the other hand, had applied lashings of a special make-up to her face to tone down the colour and shine on her skin and she had changed her top for every sequence. For, although the sequences had all been filmed in one day, they were to be spread out over five. When we eventually got to see a video of the programme, all these faults stood out. We sounded terrible. Stilted and unnatural. As if we were being forced to tell our story. At times, I even looked and sounded fed up as we had had to shoot the same sequence over and over again. We both looked puffy and waxen from exhaustion. I looked huge as I hadn't lost all the weight I had gained during pregnancy and, as I was still breast-feeding, my boobs were so big I could have gone parachuting in my bra. But, above all, we looked as if we permanently lived in one set of clothes. It was all part of the learning experience, we concluded.

When the team returned the next day, they all huddled in the kitchen again. Like the day before, the weather was cold and driech. Fortunately, there was to be no outdoor filming that day, just two indoor sequences. The first was about us and our book and the second was the dinner scene with guests, as we were required to show that we actually had some friends in our remote spot. With sheets over the windows and lit candles on the table, we filmed the evening dinner scene at eleven o'clock in the morning. This involved our guests, the uncomplaining John and Karon, and Yazzie who sat on my knee. Of course, at six months old in the middle of the morning, she didn't want to sit still and kept wriggling and babbling through the filming. And again, after a sleepless night with a restless baby and an early rise to make preparations, Jonathan and I were exhausted. However, exhaustion has never affected Jonathan's appetite and the food on the table was tormenting him. John looked as if he was having difficulty restraining himself too. When they were finally given the go ahead, they got so involved with each mouthful that, apart from appreciative noises, there was no way the producer was going to get any sense out of them. And as soon as the filming stopped, the cameraman, the sound man, and the engineer wolfed down what they could before the female contingent got a little impatient as they were expected at Moniack Castle that afternoon. With Claire Macdonald filmed before us and Moniack Castle to follow, it was good to know that our debut was in such celebrated company.

Immediately after filming at Corrunich, we headed for London. For the launch of *Classic Turkish Cookery* at the Turkish Embassy. The day after the launch we were due to fly to Turkey to research the next book in which some publishers had expressed an interest so, as Yazzie was with us and we had no one to look after her, she had to come to the Embassy too. In a bedroom, six floors up, an elderly Turkish woman had been allocated to watch over her but our country baby, who had never left my presence, apart from the few brief hours with Karon during the STV shoot, would not settle and lapsed into heart-wrenching hysterics. We had no choice but to leave her, hoping she would cry herself to sleep, as we had to attend the proceedings held in our honour with the gathered throng of journalists and food writers. But it wasn't long before the elderly woman buzzed down to say the baby was choking and needed a parent. As the author of the book, the focus of the launch seemed to be on me, so Jonathan slipped off quietly to rescue a distraught Yazzie who quietened down the minute she saw him and he carried her outside, walking her up and down the posh neighbourhood until she fell asleep on his shoulder. Only then could he rejoin the throng which had now gathered into small groups around the buffet in the dining-room. When he entered the room, he smiled at everyone and was regarded with courteous nods. As far as most people were concerned, he was a member of the security team or a waiter. The few who knew he was my husband assumed that he had come along for the ride. No one seemed to have grasped the fact that our entire book had been a joint venture and that Jonathan had taken all the photographs. That is apart from Josceline Dimbleby who told us how relieved she was that the book had turned out so well as, two years ago, she had blindly attached her name to it. It could have been a disaster, she laughed. For a writer in her position it had indeed been a gamble.

Gently Jonathan placed Yazzie over my shoulder while he fetched some food and we moved out into the less-crowded foyer where the late Jennifer Paterson, the other Fat Lady, was seated. Dressed from head to toe in shocking pink and vociferously miffed at the lack of garlic and salt in the food prepared by the Embassy chef, she immediately relieved us of Yazzie who snuggled sleepily into her large, comfortable bosom and there she remained until Jennifer was ready to don helmet and depart on her motorbike. 'Get on television,' she advised bossily as she said goodbye. 'That's where the money is. A hundred thousand plebs will see the programme and buy your book!'

After all the excitement of the publicity, our stint on television, the launch, and an invigorating trip to Turkey, our lives rapidly resumed to a low-key tempo. We were still pushing our book but, as far as the new proposals were concerned, nothing happened for a very long time. Instead we entered the game of waiting and rejection. And the slow slide into despair.

A visit from our friend David Allison, the guitar-playing BBC journalist, helped balance our thoughts. With his music, he too struggles against all odds, as he writes and produces all his own stuff. He had just finished his new guitar album, *Acoustic Movies*, and had come to us for some publicity and cover photographs. And, of course, to chew the fat. We were all feeling stressed. The recent flecks of grey in Jonathan's hair, we put down to stress. And stress seemed to have rinsed all the colour from David's hair too. With their close crops, they looked more like a pair of silver-backed gorillas. Over a few beers, Jonathan shot several reels of black-and-white film while we boosted egos. Good friends propping each other up. It all comes down to confidence. Sometimes we have it, sometimes we don't. But if the drive is there, it will all come right in the end. By the end of our group massage, we all believed in what we were doing. Then we had to live with David's face staring up at us for days as the prints were laid out on the floor to form a collage. His inspirational album included a piece entitled 'Corrunich', a beautiful little tune with a Scottish lilt that sounded like an old ballad, conjuring up many happy days together, chatting, drinking and eating in the garden. A love affair with a special place. Now every time we play the tune, the old lady beams with pride.

Quicker than expected another long winter settled around our feet. It started in October and we were neither physically nor mentally prepared for it. We had come to accept that we lived in a land of five seasons – the fifth is all of them at once, sometimes in one afternoon – and that winter is the longest season of them all but we really could have done without all the extra struggle that it entailed. The dogs were happy though, diving into snow-drifts and shovelling with their noses. They both looked so clean and fluffy and very puppyish. They didn't seem to feel the cold and the snow clung to Aslan's long fur. In between his legs, the snow collected in balls, like the baubles on a Christmas tree. We, on the other hand, were very serious. We went out sledging with Yazzie and built plump snowmen with carrot noses, but we were preoccupied with anxious thoughts. We still had no good news on our proposals. One of them, which we had called *Remote & Tasty*, was spun around the life we led and the food we ate in our remote home but editors in London were saying we couldn't possibly eat such interesting food in the highlands. That's the whole point, we screamed at the rejection letters, you can. But we were just weak voices in the wilderness. All the hope we had put into the new proposals came crashing down around us. It had been naïve of us to assume they would ride on the back of the first book. The fact was we were way out of the circuit.

Could we really keep living here? we asked ourselves again and again. We got by, but only just. Our remote cottage and others like it may still be habitable for some hardy crofters and keepers but could they really be tamed to allow our own pampered breed to lead the lifestyle we sought. Many of the local men, like Charlie the mechanic, would love to live in a cottage like ours, just like their ancestors did, but they don't because it's not practical. There are too many things stacked up against it. The hard winter for one. And the lifestyle was no longer just about the two of us, we had a child to think of. We worried that our quest for solitude would become her isolation and entertained thoughts of moving back to Edinburgh, or to the milder climate of the west coast. Better still, abroad to a scented garden where we could dive into turquoise water under a blazing sun.

But to give up at this point would have been soul-destroying and we would have regretted it for the rest of our lives. We had barely scratched the surface of our dreams. We believed we could make a living from photography and food. We still wanted to run photography workshops and we often talked about those distant dreams of working with elephants and owning a vineyard. Each project we worked on was like a building block towards the greater dream. Deep down in our hearts, we knew we had the energy and potential to pull some of it, perhaps all of it, off. We just had to convince others. If only we could rise above self-doubt and make one last attempt to hold on to our remote lifestyle.

The first step towards rehabilitation came in the form of the gregarious, if not notorious, literary agent, Giles Gordon. Already long established in London, Giles had moved back to Edinburgh so, when looking for an agent, he seemed the obvious choice. To our surprise he responded immediately and treated our proposals with enthusiasm. He had just been talking to a publisher who would have 'killed' to do *Classic Turkish Cookery*, he informed us, quoting the type of figure we should have received as an advance for such a book. A meeting was arranged and, in no time, we were caught up in Giles' whirlwind as he dispatched our proposals to publishers, talked to newspaper editors, and encouraged me to continue with the new book.

The second step was to start work on the barns. They were just sitting there, increasingly in need of repair. Jonathan had tried to fix the roofs and block up the holes but the weather always seemed to sneak in. The only creatures getting any real use out of the barns were the mice and the pigeons. We used them for storage, for wood, and for the generators but there was so much space we only required one of them. The other could adequately house a dark-room, office and studio, from where we could work on our various projects as well as commence small workshops in the future. We really did need a professional set-up. With two large dogs and an active toddler, the kitchen would no longer do. Yazzie also needed her own bedroom, the room that functioned as our office, and Jonathan, who had been kicked out of the bathroom since Yazzie was born, desperately needed a dark-room for his black-and-white work. So we got hold of Billy, the builder, and to keep the cost down, Jonathan agreed to help wherever he could.

A delivery of sand arrived in a big lorry. 'This is some place to build a house,' complained the driver, who leapt out of the cab with his bum cheeks bulging over the top of his trousers. 'Well if you get stuck, you'll have to spend the night,' Jonathan teased him. The driver shook his head with a not-on-your-life-look. No way, he was off on holiday the next day. He tipped the sand out and jumped back into the cab to drive off. No longer weighed down with its load, the lorry slid and slithered in the wet snow and the driver's face clouded in anger. He was stuck. He vented his frustration by swearing at the air and the God-forsaken place we had chosen to live in, insisting that we get him out now so he could go on his holiday. Ignoring the tirade, Jonathan fixed the tow rope to the back of the Land Rover and pulled the lorry out of the gate. 'That's some vehicle you've got there,' the driver acknowledged with relief and then asked Jonathan to pull him along the track, through the large, icy puddle to make sure he got out for his holiday. A few weeks later the same hapless driver turned up with a load of wood, his bum cheeks still poking out of the same trousers. 'Did you have a nice holiday?' we inquired, trying to be friendly. 'Aye,' he said, unloading the wood. 'Where did you go?' I asked, expecting a sunny winter location like Tenerife. 'To the pub,' he replied in a manner that indicated I was daft to even ask.

When the roe deer came down off the hills to our level, we knew we were in for a spot of trouble. Like a bullet out of nowhere, a huge dump of heavy snow landed right on top us. Trapped like ants under a giant elephant dropping, we had to tunnel our way out. There was no shifting this dump, which clung to the roof and piled into drifts like a choppy sea and remained like that for weeks. It was during this dump that Eddie, who was installing the heating in the barn, decided to bring up the hefty boiler and radiators which had been sitting in his van for days. In Tomintoul, where he lived, the snow didn't seem too bad so he headed out to us quite confidently until he reached the bottom of the track and saw that it was riddled with drifts. Clearly no one had been up or down for days. So he carried on round to Norman's to see if he could get closer to us, through his fields. When we spotted his van in the distance, struggling to keep a grip on the snow, Jonathan grabbed the sleigh and walked across the moor to help unload the heavy boiler. I bundled up Yazzie in her fleece top and trousers, strapped her into a backpack and trudged over to join them. When I got there, Jonathan and Eddie were in the process of manoeuvring the cumbersome boiler out of the van on to the sleigh by sliding planks underneath to shift it. Once it was strapped into position on the sleigh, we all pushed and shoved the bulky box, which weighed 147 kilos, through the thick, soft snow. It was hard going and beads of sweat collected around our temples. When we stopped to rest, we could feel the cold eat into our skin. Eddie, who had moved to Tomintoul from London, joked about the conditions in which we lived. 'Well, I guess we all choose where we live,' Jonathan said, philosophically. 'Yup,' agreed Eddie, with a big smile. 'That's why I live next door to a shop and a pub.'

We had just dismantled Norman's collection of broken gates, haphazardly tied together with string, and shoved the sleigh on to the open moor when it collapsed. The supports, fixed on to the skis, had given way under the weight of the boiler. And so began a long afternoon. I took Yazzie back to the warmth of the kitchen to make everyone some hot tea while Jonathan and Eddie heaved the boiler off the collapsed sleigh, which they then pulled over to the barn to fix. With two keen handymen at work, the sleigh was redesigned, sitting low on its skis, and then dragged back to the boiler which sat like a giant ice-cube in the snow. Eventually, after a great deal of effort with regular rests in between the pulling and shoving, the boiler reached its destination. 'You know there's nothing you and I can't do,' an exhausted but elated Eddie said to Jonathan. 'And anyone that says it can't be done, hasn't tried.' But the shattered mules still had the radiators to pull over.

Following a good night in the pub, where he had repeatedly recanted the story of the boiler, Eddie returned the next day to install it. Feeling a bit stiff, he had placed a few tools and his pack lunch on a sleigh, very similar to ours, and pulled it across the moor. Once he reached us he gathered up his things and handed us the sleigh. A gift. We had more use for it than he had, he explained. His father-in-law had made it some twenty years ago but Eddie had only used it once. In the woods outside Tomintoul where he went careering down a hill, over the road, and wrapped his legs around a tree. 'Almost killed myself,' he laughed. After that he had put the sleigh away for good.

In the spring *Classic Turkish Cookery* was nominated for two awards, first the prestigious Glenfiddich Award and then for the Guild of Food Writers' Award. Just the kind of boost we needed. Here was our first book, produced in remote and basic circumstances and shot on 35mm film, competing with the glossy books of famous TV personalities like Antonio Carluccio, whose genuine enthusiasm makes me positively ravenous, and the Two Fat Ladies. Holding the book in our hands, we were reminded of the sweat and tears that had quite literally gone into it. All that dragging of food through the snow, all that dancing outside to keep warm while waiting for a ray of sunlight to reflect off the mirror through the kitchen window, generators breaking down, and those long months of waiting for the book to be published. But we were reminded too of the years of research which had been a labour of love. We just hoped that the book would go some way towards lifting the dark veil under which Turkey is often surveyed and, of course, make us some money. So, in spite of the debt we had incurred, the nominations made us feel that it had all been worthwhile. We couldn't afford to go to the Glenfiddich Award ceremony in London, we barely had ten pence between us, so we phoned the publishers and asked them if they would be using this opportunity to promote the book. 'We'll ooo if you win first,' said the sales executive matter-of-factly. 'Otherwise it would be like flogging a dead horse.' Needless to say, we didn't win, it was the year of Claudia Roden, across the board, and we never heard from our publishers again. Not ones to be easily defeated though, we were inspired to milk the opportunity ourselves. We invited the press to interview us so we could air our new projects.

'Because you've got a lot of balls ringing up the nation's largest-selling newspaper,' the editor of the *Sun* told me.

'I'll run a piece. But I'd like to take the Flintstone angle.' We didn't mind. Any exposure was better than none at all. So he ran a piece entitled 'Yabadaba-dough' which gave the misleading impression that from our Stone Age cave we had produced the Flintstone cookbook. A call from a magazine agency in the south of England proved how effective the *Sun*'s story had been. The agency wanted to review the Flintstone cookbook for several women's magazines. For the first time, the local press was interested in our story, which meant that the people of Tomintoul and Glenlivet discovered what we actually did for a living. 'I thought you'd done a book on turkey feed,' laughed the postie. 'They must be loaded,' ran the gossip in the pub. And, as if she had sucked a bitter lemon, a friendly old lady in Tomintoul wrinkled her nose and shuddered as she said: 'I think what you do is very interesting but, ooh, I couldn't eat the food you eat.'

The *Sunday Times* and the *Sunday Post* both sent their journalists and photographers out to see us and ran extensive interviews. We cooked them all Turkish food and sent them home reeking of garlic. One of the photographers, who normally steered away from garlic and spices, was surprised that he actually liked the food. In fact it had been a day of surprises for him. He couldn't believe we had produced such a book from this remote location and the state of our kitchen rendered him speechless. He struggled to find a polite word to describe it. Primitive, I proffered. He agreed, thankful that I had said it, not him. When we were actually doing the book, I told him, the kitchen had been even more primitive. No fridge and a tiny camp-cooker. His eyes widened in further surprise, taking in the old pots and pans hanging above his head, the wooden shelves filled with jars of spices, and the fact that there was only enough room for the two of us. He was, he admitted, only acquainted with women who wouldn't dream of cooking a meal in a kitchen like mine. They all insisted on having fully functional, fitted kitchens. But, I explained, primitive cooking conditions had never daunted me. A few basic tools, a surface and something to cook on is all you need. I would rather spend the amount it would cost to have a fitted kitchen on travel. You must have big hearts, he remarked in wonder. It was only then that I truly understood how others saw our lives. By living here in romantic pursuit of our dreams, we really were doing something different. What we perceived to be ordinary was, in fact, a little extraordinary. But it wasn't easy. Most people, with any degree of sanity, would never voluntarily put up with half the hurdles that we endured, but we seemed to be driven by blind stubbornness and the sheer determination not to give up.

Just before the *Sunday Times* came to interview us, we attempted to spruce ourselves up a bit by getting haircuts. Our winter growth had become long and straggly, rather like the coats of the hardy ewes in Norman's field. It was April, the beginning of spring in many places, but overcast and under three-foot of snow with us. More snow was forecast for the afternoon but we decided to go to Elgin anyway. With Yazzie wrapped up in the backpack, we trudged over the moor to Norman's field where we had left the Land Rover.

Two hours later, dressed in Gore-Tex jackets and mountain boots, we arrived in Elgin where everyone was wearing T-shirts. In light bursts of liquid sunlight, a touch of spring was striking the streets of Elgin while, not far away as the crow flies, the snow was working up a storm in the wild fringes of Glenlivet. With affordable, but bad, haircuts and bags of shopping, we headed back into the shroud of a dark, wintry night to be engulfed by a whirling white-out in the Braes. We couldn't even see the edges of the road as we ploughed through the drifts. The snow closed in behind us erasing our tracks, as if it was trying to trap us in its storm. It was so wild that no one else was stupid enough to be out. We had no choice but to go forwards and try to reach Norman's farm. After blindly steering, for what seemed like an eternity, a slow course to avoid trees, fences and ditches, we eventually caught the eerie, yellow gleam of sheeps' eyes in our headlights as they huddled around Norman's barns. There were lights on in the house but no one came out. We toyed with the idea of stopping with Norman for the night but we were almost home. Temptingly close. With that thought, we plunged through the snow at great speed. The wind was so strong it rocked the car and sent swirls of snow flying into the air. We couldn't see a damned thing but we glided to the top of the field without too much difficulty.

It really was too wild to carry Yazzie in the backpack

where she would be exposed to the fierce, freezing talons of the storm so I put on her fleece over-clothes and wrapped her up, like a sausage, in my Gore-Tex jacket while Jonathan zipped into his waterproof jacket and gaiters. He then clasped the jacketed bundle tightly in his arms and, like a madman, ran as fast as he could through the sinking snow and blasting blizzard in the direction of our cottage across the moor. As I heaved the rucksack, packed with supplies, on to my back and grabbed a few extra loose bags of shopping, I could hear Yazzie's cry in the distance. It pierced my heart as I put my head down and braced the bitter night without a jacket. I too tried to run but the effort made me breathless, with a burning in my chest, as the wind buffeted my overladen body and the flurries of snow stung my face. In such a short space of time I became so exhausted and cold my teeth began to chatter like castanets. The moor had never before seemed so long and treacherous and, as there were no lights on in the cottage, only darkness lay ahead. In such conditions it is easy to misjudge distances, it is even possible to become disoriented. With the exertion, my loose trousers began to slip annoyingly down to my knees and the plastic bags swung wildly in my arms, slapping into my numbed legs. But, as I charged maniacally through the thigh-high drifts, all I could think about was Yazzie. How could we make her suffer the cold? We should never have been out in this storm. I cursed myself for the irresponsibility. All for a ridiculous, lop-sided haircut, a full inch shorter on one side, and shopping to feed a couple of comfortable, city-living journalists who would never appreciate the lengths to which we had gone.

I fell into the stream, right up to my waist, and had to crawl out on my hands and knees. The stream had come upon me sooner than I expected but at least I knew where I was now. Near the gate to Corrunich. Near to a hot cup of tea in the warm kitchen where Jonathan and Yazzie must already be. The dogs, who had run over with Jonathan, came out to escort me to the back door. I stumbled in, soaked and feeling quite weak. Jonathan, standing by the stove in the candlelight, was also soaked but Yazzie was completely dry, drinking hot tea and chatting away happily. She had cried most of the way over, Jonathan said, but mainly because her hat had slipped over her eyes and she couldn't see out of her Gore-Tex wrapping. To cheer her up, he had started to sing her 'the wheels of the bus go round and round' and, from inside the jacket, a little muffled voice had sung back 'all day long'. I was so relieved and gave her a big cuddle while Jonathan, the great protector of his little family, put on his goggles and stepped out into the blinding, stinging snow once more. He had the generator to fill and start up, followed by an arduous trek back to the Land Rover to retrieve the rest of the shopping. Early the next morning, the phone rang. It was Norman. He had just called to see if the 'wee one' had made it. It was a wild night, he said, really wild. Our windswept end of the Braes always got the beast of the storms.

*

At Easter, we woke up to the sound of mooing. Easter wasn't an occasion we usually celebrated but some have been memorable. From my childhood, there was one Easter that is firmly printed on my mind. It was in Kenya when I was eight. In the volcanic Suswa Caves, which had once been mined for their bat guano. My father, mother, brother and I tramped, very cautiously, through the dark, damp caves with thousands of squeaking bats hanging above our heads, their dung up to our knees. The high-pitched noise was almost deafening and the stench was quite nauseating but, apart from the sudden swoop of a bat into our faces, our main concern was the possibility of leopards silently lurking in darkness. Or, concealed by the thick carpet of dung, a large hole in the cave floor, dropping deep into the abyss. The old mine shafts and tracks were still there but the only signs of life were the resident colony of bats, a large family of blue-bottomed baboons, and fresh leopard spoors. My mother, who was very reluctantly taking up the rear, was having second thoughts about our little expedition, as she kept glancing anxiously behind her. So it was a huge relief when we finally emerged from the pungent gloom to the bright, hot air outside and settled down in the grass to enjoy our picnic. The baboons settled down in the grass too, near us, watching and checking each other's fur for ticks and fleas, while the big, toothy male loped around lazily and scratched his balls. My mother had cooked a deliciously lean rabbit in white wine and had brought it along in a thermos to keep it hot. Somehow, it was perfect. Bat dung, baboons, rabbit in white wine. Thinking about it now, I realise it sounds like an Addams' family Easter outing but it was certainly memorable and Elizabeth David's recipe has never tasted as good since.

With the loud mooing outside, I was about to remember this Easter too. I peered out of the bedroom window. Norman's cows had escaped again. And they were on John's land. Now that the snow had gone, the cows could smell the rotten stalks of rape that had laid dormant all winter, beneath the snow blanket. I looked over to the main gate on the track to see if it had been left open and, to my astonishment, I saw a cow jump over the fence. Then another and another. They just kept coming. Sort of hefty jumps but they managed to clear the fence. Apart from the one that jumped over the moon, I had no idea that cows were so agile. It was only about seven o'clock in the morning, far too early to disturb Norman, so we waited a few hours before calling him. By that time his whole herd was munching its way through John's field leaving tell-tale signs in the form of large droppings. Oh dear, John wouldn't be pleased. We called Norman. 'Ah, is that where they are?' Norman boomed down the phone, feigning surprise, as if he had been out all morning looking for them. 'I'd better come before John gets wind of them.' And so, in his own time, Norman dutifully strolled over to gather in his cows. There was no hurry about his pace. He lit his pipe and smoked it, while he barked a few commands at his collie and, once the cows seemed to be heading in the right direction, he came in for several large drams. Oiling his wheels, so to speak, for the stroll home.

The winter had taken its toll on our Land Rover so we took it in to Charlie's. Among other things, there was something wrong with the accelerator. I drove it in, with Yazzie and the dogs, while Jonathan followed in an old, tinny, short-wheel-based Land Rover, a 1965 Series three, that we had picked up for a couple of hundred pounds, to use as a work-horse. At Charlie's, we all piled into the old Land Rover to go back home. But, as Jonathan turned the key in the ignition, the dashboard started to spark and smoke. In a panic, I leapt out one door with Yazzie and, holding a full petrol can, Jonathan leapt out of the other and then we yanked open the back door to let the dogs out. We had visions of the old Land Rover melting before our eyes but, although it continued to smoke, it didn't actually catch fire. Charlie had a good laugh at our expense. As engines seemed to be the bane of our lives, we always managed to bring a bit of amusement to his door, and we had to return home in the lesser of two evils.

A few days later, having swapped the vehicles at Charlie's, Jonathan stopped the old Land Rover to pick up our mail at the post-box. He left it in gear as the hand-brake wasn't working but, while he was taking the mail out of the box, the engine ignited and the Land Rover drove off down the road. 'Oh, shit,' Jonathan cried out loud, barely able to believe his eyes, and he sprinted after it. Laughing and shouting at the same time, he chased it for some distance before he got a grip of the door handle on the driver's side, and still clutching the post, leapt in. 007 couldn't have done it better. As he pushed his foot down on the brake peddle, he looked around him to see if anyone had seen him. Regrettably, no one had but I had a good giggle when he told me about it. It sounded more John Cleese than James Bond. As for the cranky, old Land Rover, we didn't even bother taxing it. There were too many things wrong with it so we kept the engine ticking over for off-road driving.

Winnie the Pooh was trapped in the woods so Yazzie was taking him a pot of honey. It would keep him happy until Christopher Robin came to rescue him, she was explaining when, all of a sudden. she squealed: 'Look, Mum, people.' She said it with such wonder, as if she had caught sight of a spaceship, that the isolation of our surroundings hit me for a moment. People are a rarity. What she had just observed, though, did indeed merit some wonder. 'Good God,' I gasped, somewhat surprised, taking in the crocodile of walkers. There were about thirty of them, identically clad in bright coloured waterproofs with lunch packs on their backs. Who on earth would want to walk in the country with so many other people? The ramblers, of course. What was striking though was that, in that one group, there were more people than we had seen go by in the five years we had been living here.

In an attempt to be organic, we turned over the tough soil

which was thick with unruly weeds and nettles that tickled and stung our chins when we walked through them. To enrich the soil we scooped up the mole hills around us and John Stuart kindly gave us some of his lime, along with grass seed to thicken our patchy lawn. We also dug up some of the ancient horse manure that had been scraped out of the barns and was still in a heap on the other side of our fence. We had in fact already used some of this valuable manure as a form of currency – in exchange for the loan of a machine or a helping hand, country people are quite happy to walk off with a bag of horse shit. So with the beginnings of a vegetable patch and visions of picking salads throughout the summer, we planted a variety of lettuces and herbs, plenty of nastursiums and spinach, and onions, carrots and potatoes. As we worked outside all day, we got the feeling that we were a part of it. Aware of the sun moving around the sky, the slightest change in temperature, the whisper of a breeze, the silent arrival of a cloud of midges, and the sun slowly going down. It felt like we had all the time in the world, as if we had slowed down. So this was the farmers' secret. Now we understood why they moved like old steam engines rather than high speed trains.

For tomatoes, peppers and basil, we ordered a small wooden-framed greenhouse from England. But, as usual, the pot-holed, bumpy track turned a simple delivery into a major operation. As their truck bounced up and down, the English drivers panicked and dumped the greenhouse parts by the woods at the side of the track. Some of the glass was shattered but the drivers didn't care. They were supposed to erect the greenhouse for us but they left Jonathan to sort it out, instead. First that meant driving all the way out to Forres to borrow a horse-box from Hamish. Then he and Hamish transported the fragile compartments, two by two, along the track. Hamish drove slowly while Jonathan stood in the horse-box holding on to the glass, his heart leaping with every bump and crunch.

Meanwhile, Yazzie and I nipped down to Ladderfoot to see Pam. We had just settled down to a quiet cup of tea when Biglie and their feisty Jack Russell decided to go for one another. Of course, the Jack Russell was no match for Biglie, who clamped the entire dog in his mouth. Afraid his sharp teeth would do irreparable damage, Pam and I intervened and got bitten in the process. But Biglie did release his hold and the Jack Russell escaped with a punctured ear. Back up the track, Jonathan got bitten too. He was standing beside the last bits of greenhouse when a farm collie ran towards him, sunk its teeth into his leg, and carried on. 'He's been acting a bit strangely,' the friendly owner said as he approached Jonathan. 'I'm afraid he might bite someone.' As the blood trickled down his leg, inside his jeans, Jonathan didn't say anything. He was a bona fide highlander now. Don't complain and put up with the pain, that's their motto. They have to be dead before a doctor sees them. So Jonathan just limped for a few days while he tried to assemble the greenhouse and then strapped it down with cable so that it didn't fly away in the high winds.

*

'So were the eggs good?' Donald teased Jonathan when he came back to collect the Land Rover. Donald was a wild but jovial character who worked for Charlie. He had the build of an ox and looked like a pirate, with a disarming smile that melted his bulky features. His reputation for fighting, I was told, reached as far south as Perth. Tragically, he is no longer alive. He took his own life. No one knows why. His funeral was in the Braes, in the chapel at the bottom of our track. He was a Braes lad. It was a sad, sad day, as sombre and grey as it could possibly be. You couldn't get in or out of the Braes for the cars. People had come from far and wide. The locals felt they had been robbed.

'Come on,' Donald cajoled as Jonathan looked at him blankly. 'You're the only ones with a weird diet around here.'

It was the talk of the village. But, as usual, we didn't know anything about it. The RSPB man had taken the local bobby on to the hill to show him the empty nest of a peregrine falcon. Some eggs were missing and they were looking for heads to roll. The local joke, though, was that we had eaten them.

'It wasn't eggs that were taken,' the RSPB man corrected us a few days later, on his way into the hills. 'The chicks were killed. In a manner only possible by human hand.'

It was sad news but a regrettable reality on some shooting estates. If grouse is the currency of the Estate, some keepers will go to any length to protect them. There is so much pressure on them to produce high numbers that all other wildlife suffers. As their entire livelihood is dependent on the wishes of the Estate owner or shooting tenant, the eradication of birds of prey is a lot more common than people think. Foxes are destroyed and, in some areas, pet cats have been shot too. In this case, the RSPB man had a good idea who was responsible and, fortunately, we were not the suspects.

'I often spot you on the hill,' the RSPB man continued, looking at me.

'You do?'

'Yes. I usually hide so you don't see me.'

'Why?'

'Well, I don't want you to know where the nests are,' he answered, rather pompously. 'I used to wonder what you carried in your pack until I saw a baby's head through the binoculars.'

This information made me feel a little disconcerted. Not only had this man been behaving as if he was on some covert military operation but he had been watching me through binoculars. I couldn't begin to count the amount of times I'd dropped my pants for a pee or pulled out a breast to feed my baby. And there was that hot, balmy day I had picked blueberries in my bra. My mind boggled. I had thought I was completely alone on the hill.

When our barn was near completion, Norman was the first to come and have a peek. In muck-smeared boots, he stomped over the newly varnished floorboards and up the wooden staircase, his pipe smoke engulfing the pristine smell of wet paint.

'I wonder what old McPherson would say if he could come back from the grave,' he mused.

'He'd probably say it's a bloody waste of a good barn,' I replied, aware that all the farmers would probably think that.

'Aye,' chuckled Norman. 'He would that.'

The next to visit was John Stuart, who stopped by on his way around the fields. At one time, he had worked for McPherson and kept his cows in the barn. Now it looked unreal. Spacious and polished, with a dark-room and large studio area, it would have sat beautifully in Edinburgh or Glasgow but what was it doing out here in the middle of nowhere?

'Well, it has certainly transformed,' John acquiesced, his eyes creasing into a smile. He was too polite to say what he was probably thinking.

By the time our converted cow shed was fully functional, almost a year had elapsed. Billy, the builder, had been hindered a bit by Aslan who kept pinching his tools and bits of wood, some of which he never recovered. In fact, around the same time, a big chunk of carpet and some terracotta plant-pots mysteriously went missing too, but they were soon located. In Aslan's shit. Once Billy had finished the plastering and laying the floor in the barn, Jonathan had spent the summer painting and varnishing it, fitting in the dark-room sinks, building a retaining wall to hold back the sloping land on one side, and re-pointing the entire building. Then it was time to get a new generator. A powerful one. In five-and-a-half years, we had already been through two site generators and our third was spluttering on its last legs. In fact, it had been behaving so erratically, we had spent most of the summer without electricity. We did have a small back-up one, which our friend, Monica von Habsburg, had given us on long-term loan. 'Unless there's another war,' she had said emphatically, 'I don't need it.' As a back-up, it had come in handy but it had a petrol engine which made it expensive and inconvenient to fill as, in addition to everything else we had to bring up through the snow, it meant dragging up cans of petrol which we had to fill twenty or thirty miles away. And the engine wasn't powerful enough to run the cottage and the barn at the same time. What we really needed was mains electricity but that was still well beyond our means.

Instead, we acquired a huge, bright blue monster, which for all its size and power cost only a little more than another site generator. This was a Lister, 13kw, the next best thing to mains electricity and should have lasted us for years. That was the idea. We had thought it would be simple to install and link up to the big diesel tank. We even hoped to link it up to the cottage so that we could enjoy the luxury of turning it on and off from inside. No more reluctant trips out into the dark, freezing storms to turn off the generator and we would be able to comfort the little voice that cried out 'turn off the dark' in the middle of the night.

But, as we always find out, nothing is ever simple and the blue monster shook the cottage and the barn so ferociously we named it 'Thumper'. 'What the fuck have you got up there?' Billy teased Jonathan. 'It'll thump its way down to Norman's before you know it.' Worried about the damage the shaking could do to the old stone structures of the cottage and the barn, Jonathan had rung Billy for suggestions. We were in the process of creating our own little earthquake. Determined to solve the problem though, Jonathan entered into a long, merciless battle with Thumper, fixing the broken oil seal and the leaking fuel pump, replacing the gaskets, building a concrete base and erecting it on rubber shock-absorbers, and so the list went on, consuming him day and night until, with rattled brains, he became so tense I could have pinged him like a taut elastic band. 'I feel like I've licked a bucket of diesel,' he groaned. 'It makes me sick to the pit of my stomach.' He really was at the end of his tether and smelled like he had bathed in diesel. As he was always fixing and filling generators, it was a perpetual problem. Diesel is obnoxious stuff. It's vicious. It clings to clothes and hair and, like Lady Macbeth, Jonathan couldn't wash it off his hands. 'I don't want to live here another year with a generator,' he said with absolute finality.

An engineer came out to look at Thumper. He didn't have a lot to say and shivered in the cold air. But Charlie, who loves to have something practical to do in the open air, came up with his eldest boy to help to put on the shock-absorbers. He was in his element, enjoying the space and the view, but Thumper got the better of them all. There was no way he was going to allow a mere mortal to prevent him from shaking completely and he was so greedy, he guzzled our entire winter's supply of fuel in only a few weeks. So before the snow closed in on us, blocking the track until the spring, we had to have our fuel tank refilled and buy another site generator that would be economical to run but would probably only last a year. Another year of diesel and frustration. Another year of days, sometimes weeks, without power. And the big blue monster has had the last laugh. He is still sitting at the back of the barn, unable to budge. Now, that's what we call Thumper's revenge.

It was with an air of gloom that we accepted the inevitable snow-bound hibernation. In fact, we were so gloomy that we walked back and forth across the courtyard from the cottage to our office in the barn without ever looking at the view. Our heads were down, heavy with morose thoughts. As usual we had been trying to drum up more work with publishers, magazines and newspapers but we just couldn't seem to break through. With its vanishing act in winter, the local freelance work alone was not lucrative enough to live off so, once again, we questioned whether we should stay or not. It was becoming an annual theme. We toyed with selling up. The converted barn had increased the value of our property, so we could move with something in our pockets but, then again, did we really want to lose our home? We had put so much into it.

Couldn't we hold out a little longer? Now that we had the work premises, shouldn't we put it to good use? All we needed was a regular contract to take us through the rough winter months. Surely, that wasn't impossible. To keep our spirits up, we spent the short daylight hours organising our living, hoping our winter dilemma would go away. And it is staggering how time-consuming just living can be. There's the walking out to fetch supplies, the wood to chop and ailing machines to fix. There are gas tubes to drag up and down and vehicles to dig out of the snow. There's no end to the chores and Jonathan has to turn his hand to fixing everything. We can't just call in a plumber, electrician or mechanic, as no one would come. 'It's definitely a place for young people,' said one of our local farmers who knows the cottage well. It really is like an old lady. We have to keep her circulation going. If we neglect her, she gets damp, cold and weary very quickly.

The long winter also meant the return to months of accumulated rubbish, which we stored in the old Land Rover so that the dogs, foxes and other creatures of the night, didn't rip them apart and leave the messy inedible contents strewn over the snow. But as the old Land Rover remained stationary for so long, the mice took refuge in its shelter and bit holes in the rubbish bags, scattering the contents all over the seats instead. We repacked all the rubbish, swept out the mice droppings, and waited for a break in the storms to drive over the top of the rock-hard, frozen snow and dump the rubbish at the bottom of the track. As the heating blasted through the vents, the smell of mice filled the car. Mice under the seats, mice in the vents. Cooked mice. And then we got stuck. In a deep patch of snow that hadn't frozen. For hours, we dug and shovelled until our pipe-smoking, shaggy, winter saviour chugged up his field in his spluttering tractor and pulled us out. Backwards instead of forwards. The snow was too soft and deep ahead. And so the stinking rubbish and warm mice were reversed home for yet another spell of stench and decay.

In the middle of November, we had one of those crystal clear winter nights when the gleaming snow and moonlit shadows are so defined it's like looking at a black-and-white print coming to life in a bowl of fixer. Inside, the cottage was flooded with shafts of silver coming through the sky-light windows. There was no need for lights. And then, like a missile attack, the shooting stars skimmed across the big sky, swooped overhead and looked as if they had crashed into the hills. Some seemed to be so close that they appeared to only just clear the roof and land in the woods. We could almost touch them and found ourselves ducking as they headed towards us. Apparently no larger than a grain, these meteors had been predicted for late the following night so we wondered if we were being treated to a short preview. But the shooting stars persisted all night, some like arrows darting across the sky, some like swallows trailing a white tail, and others like fireworks exploding in a burst of pink and green with a jet-stream in their wake. They burst or popped. Every minute. Some even flashed twice and lit up the whole sky and the hills. They travelled mainly from east to west but some steered a southerly course. And when we got too cold standing in the snow, wrapped in blankets, we retreated to the bedroom and watched them through the skylight windows. It was an amazing spectacle. We had never seen anything like it and, as it only occurs every thirty-three years or so, we felt very lucky to have such clear, unpolluted skies. It was events like these that catapulted us back to the joy we had felt when we had first moved here. When we had coveted life in a remote, isolated glen. When we had enjoyed the romantic seclusion of those long winters. In those days we had been hungry for the challenge and adventure. A rollercoaster ride rather than a mundane existence. Perhaps, this meteor show would be a good omen. We should embrace the isolation and make it work for us.

In the end, it's all about fate really. Some hard work and a high dose of tenacity, but fate plays a big part. So, we started the new year with a second pregnancy, a regular food slot in a new Sunday newspaper and, a few months later, a contract for another book which had, in the way things do, evolved out of an entirely different proposal. Once again we joined the world of deadlines in the depth of our winter. Our converted cow shed was instantly put to good use as we juggled work and play with Yazzie. The short commute across the courtyard was often through a blizzard but it beat catching buses or trains, or sitting in traffic. Feeling weak and physically sick with antenatal nausea once again, I had difficulty drumming up enthusiasm to write about food and, to make matters worse, I had to cook everything we photographed. As a result, I spent a lot of time with my head over the loo and lost half a stone in weight. Needless to say, the food slot didn't get off to a good start. The photo editor was not happy with the first batch of images and made Jonathan re-photograph dish after dish, while I reeled and reeled. It was the caramelised bananas that proved the most difficult to conquer. 'They look like dog turds,' complained the photo editor, who didn't mince her words. So what was really a benign dish suddenly turned into a monster, forcing Jonathan to go through reels of film as he took a variety of photographs. Then he headed out into a fierce blizzard to walk to the car, to drive all the way to Aberdeen, where the film would be developed at a professional lab. He didn't come home that night. It was the worst weather Aberdeenshire had seen for years and the police closed the roads. Attempting a detour on his return, Jonathan flipped the Land Rover on to its side and surfed for a few metres along the edge of a lonely farm road. The windscreen was smashed but he was unhurt. A local farmer pulled him out but there was no way he could reach the Braes of Glenlivet that night so he double-backed to Huntly. The next day, tired and hungry, he drove the wounded vehicle to the bottom of the track and trekked home through the snow. He had posted the film and met the photo editor's deadline but, if it hadn't been for those bananas, he would never have been out in such a storm.

And, to cap it all, the photo editor ran with the original 'dog turd' shot.

'Where the hell have you been?' Norman growled, as he heaved open the gate to his field.

'Staying with the grandparents,' we replied, feeling a little guilty, aware that it was a sign that our reserves were weakening.

We had had heavy colds and had inflicted ourselves on my parents for a few days to give Yazzie a change of scene while we got better. Living the way we do, it's difficult enough when one of us is down with a bug but when both of us are feeling absolutely lousy it's practically impossible. Corrunich is such a physical place, it relies on both of us being on our feet.

'That wasn't very neighbourly of you,' he chastised gruffly.

What he meant was that he had been worried about us in the storms. When he had gone out in his tractor and seen that there were no lights on in Corrunich and no signs of life, he had grown genuinely concerned. We would let him know the next time, we reassured him. And he beamed as he lit his pipe. He had made his point. Now it was time for a puff and a chat. In the winter, there is no escaping the hard isolation. Company is in short supply.

I was upstairs in the cupboard being a hairy giant when I heard voices downstairs in the kitchen. I wondered who it could be. Much to the disappointment of little Yazzie, I came out of my hiding place and crept down the stairs. The dogs hadn't barked and I could hear Jonathan's voice, punctuated by laughter, so I presumed it was someone we knew. It must be Hamish and Pam, I thought, as no vehicles can get up the track. They must be walking down to Ladderfoot. But when I entered the kitchen, only Jonathan was there. He was having a complete conversation with himself. We laughed about it but it did make us wonder. Were we so isolated that we were going mad? Mad or recluse? In the end, one probably leads to the other.

Aside from the possibility of going mad, we often say we would like to live somewhere much more remote. Where the mail is delivered by seaplane. We're kidding ourselves, of course. We have enough difficulty coping with living here in the winter. But, when the storms clear away and the winter struggles are over, and the scene around us fills with light and laughter, we focus on the good moments. The winter wasn't that bad, we say. In fact, we enjoyed the challenge and isolation. And now that the loneliness of winter is behind us, we have company again. Norman's burly figure becomes a familiar sight on the horizon or at our back door; John, astride his quad, regularly checks his fields, exchanging a few friendly words here and there; Hamish and Pam pop down to Ladderfoot where we frequently sort out the world over a few drinks; and friends can get up the track and we can get down.

But, as the years go by in our highland outpost, we are not fooled. This really is a hard place to live and a hard place to make a living. Bare, bleak country, tinged with clear, magical light. For the romantic, that is its beauty. And, at times, it is staggeringly beautiful. For the dweller though, struggle is undoubtedly its soul. Such has been the exodus from this area that where there was a school of one hundred pupils, now there is none. Today, there are only a handful of children in the Braes. In-comers come and go and a high percentage of the population live below the poverty line. People are happy enough if they can just get by. And, to do that, they need to have their fingers in several pies. For example, a mechanic doesn't just fix engines. He must be a fireman, a member of the mountain rescue team, a stand-in bus driver, and experienced at plumbing, fencing and lambing. With few funds for education and living, areas like these will slowly die. It's the Clearances all over again, lament some of the locals. Only the very tough, those that have been born into this life, will survive.

Our second child very nearly didn't survive. He was born ten days late and, once again, after a long and difficult labour, I was strung up on the theatre slab for a forceps delivery. But the baby got stuck with his head turned upwards. The obstetrician prepared us for the worst. He was going to have one more go at delivering the baby with forceps. If that didn't work, he would have to perform a Caesarean. As the baby was too far up for the forceps and too far down for a successful Caesarean, there was a chance the baby might not survive.

This was almost more than we could bear. We had been so looking forward to having another baby and to giving Yazzie a brother or sister. And, on the run up to the birth, we had felt we had really messed her around as I had been in and out of hospital with false labours. She had come to dread the sight of my overnight bag being put into the car every time we left home. 'Are you going to leave me again?' she would say quietly, the tears welling up in her eyes. She had clung on to me, night and day, in the hope that I wouldn't go away. When I did go into labour again, nine days past the expected date of delivery, we had barely been able to get down the track, the contractions were coming so fast and furiously. We had swung by the doctor's surgery first and he phoned the hospital. He had to practically twist the obstetrician's arm to take me in. My cervix wasn't sufficiently dilated, so the obstetrician wasn't overly concerned. But, said our doctor, there's no mistaking the contractions and given the distance, he really felt I should be in hospital. So we had set off to Aberdeen, via Braemar. A somewhat circuitous route from Tomintoul but we had to leave a hysterical Yazzie with my parents. My heart had wept for her, she was so tired and confused, but I knew she was in the best place she could be as it might be a long time before Jonathan could go back for her.

The farms and hills had flashed by as we meandered through Aberdeenshire to the labour ward. My parents had lent us their mobile phone, so we called to see how Yazzie was doing. She was fine, dressing up and chatting.

Children are so resilient. So we had concentrated on getting to hospital on time. The contractions were coming every two minutes and we hit rush hour outside Aberdeen. I really hoped I wasn't going to have a difficult time. Surely, it wouldn't be long before the baby was born. But our second baby was reluctant to come out too and my labour followed the pattern of the first. Long, agonising, and exhausting. All conducted in the most ridiculously small gown. There wasn't a shred of dignity, I was barely covered. But that was to be the least of the problems

From my paralysed, horizontal position, with a dozen or so faces peering down at me, I watched the obstetrician pull and heave with the forceps. With teeth clenched and the veins in his neck at bursting point, the strain on his face was almost painful to watch. It was surreal. Boy George was blasting out of the speakers, the obstetrician looked as if he was delivering a stubborn calf, the green gowns and masks were watching with medical interest, and Jonathan and I held on to each other for dear life, hoping our baby would be all right. I could barely hold back the tears. What would I say to Yazzie if I returned home with no baby? Suddenly, the obstetrician sprang a bloody mass on to my stomach, as if he had landed a whopping big fish. It was a fine, healthy baby boy with large nostrils and a crumpled ear.

Once again it was lovely to get home to the fresh air and space. Away from the hospital heat, the clinical smells, and the constant prodding. In the recovery ward I had been put in a bed next to a fifteen-year-old, who was blooming and comfortable, dressed to leave, after a straightforward four-hour labour. Her mother, who was on hand to help, was younger than I was. It had made me feel positively wracked and geriatric. And when little Yazzie had arrived later with her dad, she had been a bit disappointed at the sight of her baby brother. He was sleeping in a plastic cot, with his hair still matted with blood. He didn't just sit up and say hello. She had dolls that were more animated. But once he was home, feeding and crying, he seemed real. When she thought I wasn't looking, she gave him the odd thump but, secretly, she liked him and generously piled her most unsuitable toys on top of him. We named him Zeki, another Turkish name that we hoped would cross all divides.

Shortly after Zeki's birth, we parted company with our old Land Rover. Without a major overhaul, it was no longer of any use as an off-road vehicle. It really was on its last legs. To fix it for our own use would have cost more than it was worth, so Charlie said he would see if he could make it roadworthy and sell it to recoup some of the money. That, of course, meant Jonathan had to drive it into Tomintoul. It coughed and spluttered and blew its exhaust in through the windows before it careered off up the track. It was off. But Jonathan couldn't stop it. The brakes didn't work at all. At the bottom of the track, he drove through the stream to avoid a tractor and toppled, bumpity bump, on to the road. From there he had a straight run into Charlie's. No halting vehicles, no sheep or cows being herded along the roads, no oncoming cars at the Pole Inn turning, in fact, no reason to stop at all. He was very lucky. But, at Charlie's, he had no choice. He had to stop. Down the slight hill he went, in first gear, but there was a tractor in the way. He couldn't stop. So he drove on by, waving at Charlie's boys. Up through Tomintoul, he drove, and back down to Charlie's. There was still a tractor in the way. So he drove on by, waving at Charlie's boys. Up and back down again. The tractor had moved and a keeper's Land Rover was now blocking the entrance. So he drove on by, waving at Charlie's boys. By this time, they thought he was mad. Changing his approach tactic, the madman turned right and drove out of Tomintoul to a layby, where he drove straight into a tree, right beside a family of tourists having a picnic. Having managed to successfully stop the runaway Land Rover, he calmly reversed to turn it round, and gave the family a cheery wave. They watched him, astonished. These highlanders are strange, they must have been thinking, they don't even use their brakes. Then the old Land Rover made its final limp uphill and came to a controlled halt just outside Charlie's.

A few weeks later, our ongoing battle raised its bothersome head. Right in the middle of an act of sheer decadence, dipping chunks of fresh bread into a gooey, melted camembert, the power cut out. Spiked with garlic and a dribble of white wine, just as Nigel Slater had suggested, the camembert had been baked in its box. It was deliciously warm and had to be eaten immediately, otherwise it would stick to the inside of the mouth like glue. But the generator has a knack of invading such special moments. So we lit a candle and finished the camembert before dealing with the generator. A degree of enjoyment had been snatched from us, though. We knew it was serious. We knew that the generator had well and truly packed in. It would have to go down to Glasgow to be fixed and, in the meantime, we would have to resort to our only link with electricity. Thumper. That wretched, greedy, blue machine. It was Sod's law when the snow fell down the next day. In one big dump, it blocked us in. So, once again, we were faced with dragging the generator through the snow. By the time we got the generator back we had almost run out of diesel. Thumper had greedily guzzled the winter's supply. Just when we needed electricity more than ever, with our increased workload and a new baby.

So why do we stay? People often ask us this. Wouldn't it be easier to live in the city and come to the cottage for weekends? Maybe. But now that we've had a taste of the wilderness and isolation, it's difficult to step out of it. I love reminding myself that we live in a place other people come to for their holidays. I feel that, here, we're actually living every moment of our lives, not just letting it pass by. And, although it can be hard, there really is never a dull moment. It's a bit like living abroad. Before coming here, I knew Turkey and Italy far better than my own homeland. It has taken time to get to know people. We've had to adapt. We've had to learn to take things as they come. And we don't take ourselves too seriously. The highlands would never allow us to. I do wonder, from time to time, if we will ever be able to fulfil our dreams of photography workshops, documentary films, elephants and the vineyard. But then I think, what's the hurry? Right now, we're stretched from dawn until all hours of the night, just trying to manage our work and our children. Completely on our own. For out here, there is no one to help.

When things get on top of us, as they do, and we find our lifestyle bullied and threatened by things like generators and a lack of funds, we climb the hills to take an eagle's view of our little world. It never fails to put things into perspective. Inspired and liberated by that elusive feeling of space again, there are few places we would rather be. This is our spiritual home. Our fire and our soul. It makes us laugh and it makes us cry. It is a place to which we have made a commitment. We've planted rowans, aspen, and bird cherry for shelter, we've started a garden and begun to make it look homely, and we really miss it whenever we leave for any period of time. So strong is its magnetic pull, we often say that if we ever win the lottery we would stay here. Of course, we're not completely daft, we would put in mains electricity or wind power and we would buy a tractor or skidoo to ease the passage of winter, as the one thing that worries me is that we can't get out with ease or speed in an emergency and there is school to think of. But, if we can, we shall stay. For here, in the depth of the highlands, more than any other place we know, we can give our children the chance to run free in the wild open spaces. And, to us, that's the biggest dream of all.

We spent Christmas in Braemar. On a good day, it is only an hour away over the hills. But, when we returned home on Boxing Day, the hilltop road was blocked with snow, so we had to take a long detour. Once we reached the Braes, there was noticeably more snow than anywhere else and the track up to our cottage was completely filled in. We had to give it a try so we speeded up and launched into the snow. It was too deep, over the Land Rover's bonnet. With a three-year-old and three-month-old baby on board, we solemnly accepted defeat. We reversed out and headed round to Norman's. Not like the old days when we would have got stuck and then spent the rest of the day digging the car out of the snow and making several trips up and down the track to get all our gear back home.

There was no sign of Norman and Jean but we knew, by now, that they wouldn't mind us driving up through the field. With the car filled with the dogs and their beds, bags of warm clothing, a huge pack of nappies, a case of wine, and all the children's cumbersome Christmas presents, we were keen to get as near to our door as possible. We surfed up to the top of Norman's field and stopped by the fence. Just on the other side was John Stuart in his tractor. He had been feeding the sheep in his field, which was sheltered by the plantation. We waved and Jonathan hopped over the fence to wish him a happy Christmas.

The weather was bright but it was cold and windy. John could see that, with children, we could do with a hand and offered to take us over to our cottage in his tractor. As I climbed into the back with the children and perched on a bale of straw, he apologised for the stench of manure. Then John sat in the seat and Jonathan, hunched over by the low cab roof, supported himself beside him. With straw in the cab and manure in the dumper, there was no room for any of our luggage, so we set off slowly through the snow as the big tractor wheels carved out two deep tracks with ease. Obviously, we needed one of these, I was thinking. A second-hand, four-wheel-drive tractor. It was as slow as a snail and tipped precariously on some of the uneven drifts but it was solid and thorough and relatively warm. We would be able to get the children to school and we would be able to get down the track in an emergency. The snow was so deep it was above the high tractor wheels and it had buried the gate that led on to the moor. Jonathan and John shovelled away some of the snow and lifted the heavy, wooden gate off its hinges to let the tractor through. The gate to our home was also buried so John stopped outside it. We thanked him. He had made it easy for me with the children and my wobbly, sore hips which had still not repaired since Zeki's birth. Then he waited for Jonathan to pick up the sleigh and took him back to the Land Rover. While I got the children and the cottage warm, Jonathan hauled everything over. Several trips later, with darkness falling around us, we were all back in the cosy bosom of Corrunich. The stove was lit, the hot water was on, the dogs, pleased to be home, were sleeping peacefully in their beds, and we were drinking steaming mugs of sweet, milky tea. It had taken just over eight hours to get ourselves and our belongings home. It would have taken longer if John hadn't been in his field with the tractor. And it would have been tough on the children if it had been blowing a blizzard. But it was bad enough that a one hour journey had taken eight hours, so Jonathan and I made a pact that, while the children were so young, we would just stick to our guns and have Christmas at home.

'I hope the ceremony goes better than the launch of *Classic Turkish Cookery*,' Jonathan said to a friend we were having dinner with in London.

We had come down for the annual Glenfiddich Food and Drink Awards, the Oscars of the food world. This time Jonathan had been short-listed for his photographs in the *Sunday Herald*. We couldn't really afford to come but, equally, we couldn't afford to miss the opportunity to meet the editors and celebrities of the food world. We had always felt that we were out of the circuit and never got any feedback on our work, so here was the chance to meet and be seen. Somehow, I was going to squeeze my extra bulk into some pre-pregnancy number that had been hanging in the cupboard for months. Jonathan, on the other hand, was going to look trim and smart in his only suit, which he had had made in Turkey. With his dark silvery hair, his beard and moustache, he looked a touch

European or Middle Eastern. Just as he had done at our book launch.

'Why?' asked the friend, shovelling pasta into his mouth. 'What happened at the launch?'

'Nobody knew who I was,' Jonathan recounted with a smile. 'And because it was held in the Turkish Embassy, all the press and celebrities there thought I was a waiter or one of the security guards.'

'Well, you should make sure the launch of your next book is in the Norwegian Embassy!' laughed the friend.

Jonathan didn't win the Glenfiddich Award And nobody thought he was a waiter or security. In fact, nobody knew who we were. So, with our reserves emboldened by the flowing champagne, we entered the sophisticated throng and introduced ourselves to all the people we recognised by face or name. The fact that Jonathan had been short-listed out of all the food photographers across the board made us feel that even we, in our little highland outpost, were part of the bigger picture. Perhaps we were getting somewhere at last. The photographer who did win commented that food photographers never work alone and have a whole team of people, including an art director, food stylist, and home economist to thank. However, if Jonathan had won, his list would have been short. It's just the two of us. I cook and Jonathan shoots. It will either be our success, because we're different, or our downfall.

We were soon back to our reality in the distant hills to find a sprinkling of fresh snow on the ground and the delicate, paper-thin narcissi dancing in the sunny breeze. Our trip to London seemed unreal. It was far, far away. We had the dogs to feed and the children to put to bed. Then we lit the stove and settled down to a simple supper of the Big Yin's eggs. The Tomintoul shop had increased its highland fare to include eggs from Billy Connolly's freerange hens, just a skip over the hills. With work short-listed for an award, the murmuring of new projects on the horizon, and a regular supply of fresh, tasty, orange-yoked eggs, life in our remote glen was definitely looking up.

Not long after our seventh Corrunich anniversary, Shan arrived to stay. We had seen him on our occasional jaunts to London, and we often spoke on the phone, but it had been seven years since he had set foot in our glen. In fact, it had been seven years since he had set foot in Scotland. His time was divided between London and India. He looked as slick and fashionable as ever when he stepped off the plane, decked out in Armani, with his toothbrush in his pocket. He was only coming for one night. It was all he could spare from his hectic, stressful property-developing business. And it was all he could handle in the country.

'Man, what a lot you've done to the place,' he said in amazement, as he looked around the cottage and barns. New roofs, new windows and doors; re-pointed walls, harled gable-end and lots of hardcore; pots of herbs, a vegetable garden and greenhouse; Wendy house and a sand-pit. 'It's so homely, as if you've been here for years.'

Seven years. Oh, my God. Where had it all gone?

Shan's last visit seemed like yesterday. We had got a few things off the ground and we had brought two children into our world, but the time had just zoomed by.

'I can't believe you're still here, man,' Shan laughed, later on that night. He was outside looking through the dark at the view, dimly lit by a shrouded moon, while Jonathan poured diesel into the generator. The night air was a bit nippy, eating its way through the thin layer of Armani. He was shivering as he laughed. His wonder had gone up an octave. 'There's nothing out here, but the fucking moon, man!'

As he climbed into the Land Rover the next day, Shan took one last look at the place. Sadly, his visit was over and Jonathan was going to drive him back to the airport. So, from the comfort of the car seat, the property-developer's eyes feasted.

'You know, I wouldn't mind buying a place like this,' he exclaimed, suddenly, with excitement. 'It would be great for weekends.'

Time Warner Paperback titles available by post:

☐ The Olive Farm	Carol Drinkwater	£7.99
☐ The Olive Season	Carol Drinkwater	£7.99

The prices shown above are correct at time of going to press. However, the publishers reserve the right to increase prices on covers from those previously advertised without prior notice.

_____ **timewarner** _____
paperbacks

TIME WARNER PAPERBACKS
P.O. Box 121, Kettering, Northants NN14 4ZQ
Tel: 01832 737525, Fax: 01832 733076
Email: aspenhouse@FSBDial.co.uk

POST AND PACKING:
Payments can be made as follows: cheque, postal order (payable to Time Warner Books) or by credit cards. Do not send cash or currency.

All U.K. Orders	**FREE OF CHARGE**
E.E.C. & Overseas	25% of order value

_____

Name (Block Letters) _____

Address_____

_____

Post/zip code:_____

☐ Please keep me in touch with future Time Warner publications

☐ I enclose my remittance £_____

☐ I wish to pay by Visa/Access/Mastercard/Eurocard

Card Expiry Date

_____